I0081916

HINTS FOR PROSPECTORS

Hugh Corbet

ETT IMPRINT

Exile Bay

This 11th edition published by ETT IMPRINT, Exile Bay 2025

First published in Australia in 1932 by the West Australian Mint as *Hints for Prospectors and Owners of Treatment Plants*. Revised and reprinted 1933 (twice), 1934 (twice), 1935 (twice) , 1946, 1947, 1960.

New edition published by ETT IMPRINT in 2025
First ebook published by ETT Imprint in 2025

ISBN 978-1-923205-63-5 (pbk)
ISBN 978-1-923205-64-2 (ebk)

Design by Tom Thompson

Cover: Alluvial Digger's Claim, Kanowpa, 1900. Detail of a photograph by J.J. Dwyer, courtesy of the West Australian Government.

Contents

Prospecting for Gold

Miner's Rights

A Miner's Right is required before a person can prospect for gold or minerals. It can be obtained from the Mines Department, Perth, or from any Mining Registrar on the Goldfields upon payment of a fees and upon the full name of the applicant being supplied.

After you have decided on the district you intend to prospect, you should equip yourself to meet the conditions you are likely to encounter. Not to be well informed and well equipped is a large handicap to carry. When it comes to the actual prospecting it must not be forgotten that most of the easily found gold, both reef and alluvial, has already been discovered, and therefore a modern-day searcher must be prepared to expend more patience and be more thorough in his search than his predecessors.

Having gone so far as to be equipped with a miner's right, a pick and shovel, compass, dolly pot and screen, prospecting dishes (2), hand magnet, water carriers (water hags, etc.), and possibly some form of shaker or dryblow- ing machine, and with his personal camp equipment the prospector should have enough for a start. Explosives, hammers, drills and bellows, etc., could come after something has been located worthy of developing. The next question would be to arrange for transport. A few lessons in camp cooking will do no harm.

The prospector, having reached his objective, should first make sure of his water and food supply. By neglecting these items in the early stages much time is lost and much energy wasted.

A well-arranged and comfortable camp will help the prospector to keep fit and in good health. A bed of bags and bush timber can he quite restful even if it is not ornamental. The tent can be shaded by a canopy. The water-bag can he kept cool by being in complete shade and at the same time exposed to whatever wind there is. Arrangements for cooking should be simple, practical and safe.

When established as far as possible with the necessaries as enumerated above, prospecting should he carried on in some methodical manner, so as to cover an area hit by hit and thoroughly. Of course gold may he found by walking around and just "trying out" patches haphazardly; it often has been, hut as most success in life is obtained by systematic action, probably the same will hold good as far as prospecting is concerned.

Therefore, the advice is to resort to your map. Choose an area and start the search to suit the fancy, hut let it he systematic.

The question of choosing an area to prospect will give the newcomer some anxiety, hut the following points may be noted. Remote areas require good transport and extensive supplies. An old mining field nearer at hand may offer better chances to the novice. He will see what is done, and how, and he will meet experienced miners. Gradually he will he more fitted to make the adventure, outback, if that remains his ambition.

In choosing the area, a prospector would be well advised if he confined his energies to the greenstone areas and very old sediments. Furthermore, gold is more likely to occur in foliated or schistose greenstone than in the more massive blocky types. Really, in planning a prospecting campaign one should make a study of geological maps and bulletins, but this must be recognised as not always practicable.

In the first place try not to go over the same ground twice. Test every outcrop you come to, whether it be rock, reef or lode, by sampling, crushing and panning off; loam any ground on a slope which is descending from a reef or lode material. If there is any gold about you should at least find traces. When once a trace of gold is found, particularly on a slope, follow it up as a dog will a scent and trace it to where it disappears. Then search on that spot until the origin is discovered. Do not waste too much time on flat ground, particularly if it is "deep" ground, unless gold has been found in the surrounding hills, and particularly if that gold occurred in rich leaders. In this State deep leads are seldom, if ever, found very close to big mines. Most rich leads are derived from the gold shed from rich stringers; good examples being those at Kalgoorlie, where the Venture Lead can he traced to Cassidy's Hill; Kanowna, where the North Lead evidently originates from quartz stringers in Tom Doyle's Hill, and so on.

Take every precaution, when you locate gold, to mark the spot, so that it can he easily found again. Much time and many opportunities have been lost in looking for the " lost find."

Finally, if the prospector has been lucky enough to find gold he should immediately peg out and apply for a Prospecting Area or Lease.

Regulations

The area of ground which may he pegged as a prospecting area for gold or minerals is as follows:-

(a)   Outside the limits of a Goldfield or Mineral Field, or more than 50 miles from the nearest mine - 48 acres.

(b)   Within the limits of any such Field - 24 acres.

Every mining tenement shall be taken possession of and marked off by fixing firmly in the ground at each corner or angle thereof a substantial post or cairn of stones projecting not less than three feet above the surface and set in the angle of two trenches, not less than four feet in length and six inches deep and cut in the general direction of the boundary lines. When the nature of the ground will not permit of trenches being cut, rows of stones of similar length shall be substituted. The boundary lines shall also be cleared from post to post.

One of the corner posts or cairns shall be the datum post, and thereon shall be firmly fixed at the time of marking off, a notice in the Form No. 22 in the Schedule of the Mining Act, 1904.

Applications for registration of any mining tenement shall be made on the prescribed forms within ten days after marking off. The forms can be obtained from any Mining Registrar or from the Mines Department, Perth.

Such application, together with a sketch of the ground applied for, must be lodged at the office of the Mining Registrar. of the particular Gold or Mineral Field wherein the ground is situated, and must be accompanied by the necessary fees.

When any holder of a mining tenement decides to abandon his holding it is obligatory upon him to lodge a surrender of his title. with the Mining Registrar. If this is not done, the holder renders himself liable to the infliction of a fine.

Form 22.   M.D. 93. WESTERN AUSTRALIA Reg. 148.
The Mining Act, 1904
Notice of Marking off a Mining Tenement other than a Lease

NOTICE IS HEREBY GIVEN THAT * I, John Brown, the under-signed, of Southern Cross, have this day, at the hour of 10 o'clock a.m., marked off this land as a the Prospecting Area for Gold under the provisions of "The Mining Act, 1904." The dimensions of the ground intended to be applied for are twenty-four acres and the following is a description of the boundaries thereof :
(Here set out particulars.)
        Datum peg being one chain South-West of the South-West corner of Gold Mining Lease 2345.
        Thence 12 chains East
        20 chains South
        12 chains West
        20 chains North
        back to datum peg.
Dated this 9th day of August, 1945.

Miner's Right No....
* I or We.

Date 7/8/1945

John Brown
Signature of Applicant.
Place of Issue
Southern Cross

* Here state particulars of the mining tenement to be applied for

Marking Out an Area

The Mining Act requires that whenever possible a mining tenement shall be laid out as a rectangle. Careless pegging has sometimes caused trouble, and the following method of pegging a right angle is very useful:-

Fix two posts and thus define one side. From either post measure back along the boundary line a distance of

The prospecting of ground is of the utmost importance. The results in three yards, and mark the spot with a small peg. A point on the line at right angles to the first side will be four yards from the corner post and five yards from the smaller peg. (Note - Greater accuracy will be obtained by using distances greater than three yards, four yards, and five yards as stated above, and any distances which are in the ratio three, four, and five will do.)

The normal area allowed to the prospector is 24 acres, and it is fairly generous. He should make the best use of it by marking out the line of the lode or reef that is to be worked, and then arranging a margin reckoned safe. The limitations are that the prescribed area (in this case 24 acres) shall not overlap anyone else's pegging, that it shall be rectangular and that its length shall not be greater than twice its width.

A convenient size is 12 chains by 20 chains, or 264 yards br 440 yards.

Assuming that the lode runs North and South, let us mark first the Western boundary of our area. The other boundaries will have to conform to this so we must be careful. Let us place the Western boundary six chains West of the assumed line of the lode or reef. This line and this boundary should be cleared. We have still to fix the position of the North-West and South-West pegs. These pegs should be 20 chains apart. Marking off areas has been carried on for many years, but few prospectors have measuring facilities that a surveyor would regard with patience. Prospectors have trusted mainly to pacing, and that will be the only available method in most cases still. We will fix our North-West and South-West pegs as nearly as possible 20 chains (440 yards) apart. Let us be sure that this boundary is where we want it. (See Fig. 2.)

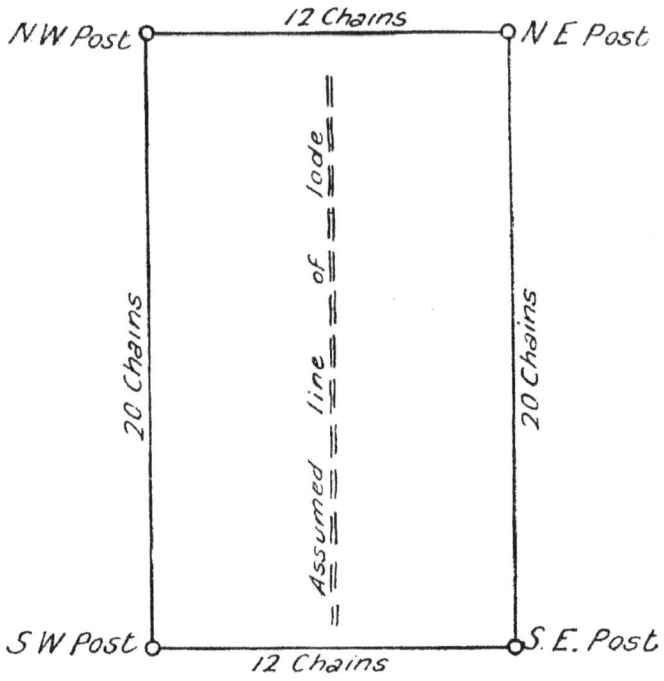

Fig. 2

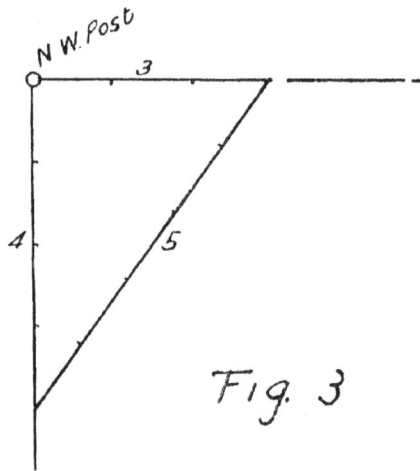

Fig. 3

The next stage is to mark the North boundary, which is to be at right angles to the West boundary.

Let us take the North-West post as the datum post. We have now to set off a right angle. (See Fig. 3.)

From the North-West post measure-off four units of length along the West boundary. Ten feet would he a good unit, and if you can get a fairly straight stick about ten feet long that will do for the unit. Four units along the North boundary from North-West post, put in a peg. (It will be understood that for finalising the angle pacing is not accurate enough, though it can be used to roughly set out the position of the three-unit peg.)

Now measure off in an Easterly direction three units, and insert a peg. If this three-unit peg is now found to be five units from the four-unit peg, then the three-unit peg is on the North boundary, and the angle at North-West post forms a right angle. If the distance between two pegs is more or less than five units, then the three-unit peg is in the wrong place, and must be shifted. Its correct position is three units from the North-West post, and five units from the four-unit peg. If the prospector has three cords respectively three units, four units, and five units long, it can be understood that the setting out of the right angle is greatly facilitated.

Along a line from the North-West Post through the three-unit peg to the North-East Post is the North boundary of our area. The North boundary is to be twelve chains (264 yards) long, and a Post is to mark the North-East corner.

Now from the South-West Post (at the South end of the West boundary) with similar method, set out the Southern boundary.

The angles at the four corners of the area are to be marked with trenches not less than four feet long and six inches deep.

The boundary lines are to be cleared from post to post.

The four corner posts or cairns are to be substantial and firmly placed.

On the North-West or datum post place a notice (Form 22) of which an example has already been given.

The position of the datum post is to be described as accurately as possible by bearing and distance from a natural feature, Mining Lease, or surveyed point.

Exploring a Project

To prove the value of a prospect at a minimum cost, confine all preliminary work to the ore body. In sinking, follow the variations of the lode or reef to, say, a depth of 50 or 100 feet, in order to prove whether the values are superficial or not. Do not attempt to select a site for a shaft before first ascertaining the value and position of the ore body at that depth. The dip of a lode may be sharply reversed within those horizons and a shaft sunk from the surface may prove to be practically useless at even a very moderate depth. Difficulties of haulage are easily overcome by the intelligent construction of skidways made from bush timber. Remember that a shaft sunk in the country is simply a hole in the ground, whilst an excavation on the lode is of definite value for the examination and. sampling of the deposit. Do not overlook the requirements of safety - the shaft you are sinking may have to be timbered, especially in weathered rock.

LEVER . SINKING SHAFT.

Sinking a mine Shaft in Bendigo, 1853 by RW. Jesper (National Library of Australia).

Prospecting Hints for the New Man

Get a mate with experience and spend some time with experienced men, and profit by what you see and hear (though there is no necessity to believe all you hear).

It is waste of time and money to start off scratch by yourself. You cannot expect, in a few days, to acquire knowledge that has taken other men years to acquire.

When proposing to operate in a district, assuming it a prospector should first acquaint himself with the characteristics of the local ore bodies, whether there are certain minerals usually associated with gold, or whether the payable deposits are to be found in the form of contacts, shoots with a sharp downward trend, flat lenses, and so on. In most cases this can be readily learned by consultation with prospectors who have a practical knowledge of the district.

Kookynie district might be taken as a striking example. Around Kookynie proper, for a radius of a couple of miles, the minerals most looked for in association with gold are oxide of iron and iron pyrites. About five miles to the north, in what is known as the Britannia line, galena is the indicator of values, while four miles south, at Niagara, bismuth is usually associated with payable ore, and oxide of iron, and iron pyrites seldom indicate values. The nearest mining camp towards the east is Yerilla. There, manganese is the mineral associated with the higher grade ore, yet adjacent to Kookynie manganese spells poverty. At Menzies the gold is frequently associated with galena and zinc blende.

All favourable places have been tried and worked with more or less success, and it is mostly these that are now receiving attention.

Gold is not easily found. But if the present day prospector works hard and intelligently he will make enough to live on, and perhaps a little more, and he will always have the chance of a rich find.

Don't shift camp too readily; first consider the surface indications and, if they are favourable, make a thorough test for a distance of at least $1^{1/2}$ miles from camp in all directions. After heavy rains look for surface gold, examine for any floaters, and ascertain by dollying if they contain gold and mineral. They may indicate that values exist below the surface soil and decomposed country rock. Be patient in loaming and, if traces of gold are found, costean for values in close proximity, then sink on a vein or lode and follow values; even when given out, continue sinking, if indications are favourable. Keep the dolly pot going, and clean it after each sample, by crushing in it some barren quartz.

Never attempt to go down any abandoned shaft that has no connection to another shaft. It may contain the foul air called carbon dioxide. Lower one or two candles, either in a bucket or petrol tin, to the bottom. If they remain alight this shaft is free from carbon dioxide. Even when sinking a new shaft in very flat and heavily timbered country repeat these precautions every day. To overcome this danger, divide shaft with brattice cloth or thick hessian just behind ladder end, leaving about eighteen inches for travelling way. Be careful not to set fire to brattice cloth when travelling up or down ladders.

Never descend an old shaft that has the "rotten egg" smell of Hydrogen Sulphide, a highly poisonous gas that has caused the deaths of many miners. First shovel lime down the shaft and then blow the foul air out with a wind sail.

When using a rope to climb with, see that it is not rubbing on a cutting edge. In old workings there may be loose ground, broken timber, snakes, or accumulations of poisonous gases. When handling explosives do not smoke. Do not carry loose caps in your pockets. Be careful about Kerosene - it maybe petrol. Be cautious about what you find in old trapping camps - often enough the stuff in the baking powder tin is arsenic. Beware of a gun at any time, but especially when you think it is not loaded. "There is nothing so dangerous as an unloaded gun." Never enter old mine workings unless you have a mate present.

Do not venture into new country that is timbered or very flat without first taking your hearing from the sun and a watch to indicate the time you travel in a certain direction. Do not venture too far until you become acquainted with the hush. When in breakaway-country do not attempt to wander in it without a reliable compass.

Always he observant: rich finds are got mostly by careful observation. If indications puzzle you, seek advice before abandoning any area taken up. Ascertain from the School of Mines or Geological Survey the nature of rock by sending in rock samples for determination. Do not accept hearsay evidence that the district is patchy and difficult. Persevere and you may discover values exist in most unexpected places and in strata different from any yet observed by others.

Gold occurs in Western Australia as alluvial or lode deposits.

A Geologist's Notes

(Many of the old prospectors, before they venture into new country, get all the available evidence, not only from brother prospectors, hut from Bulletins of the Geological Survey, and from the Geological map of the State.)

1.   **Alluvial.** - Alluvial gold is usually traceable to the shedding of gold from quartz veins and ironstone leaders. In some cases it may be due to the precipitation in alluvial ground of dissolved gold. Alluvial gold of both kinds is most usually found in greenstone country. Instances of finding gold in old sediments as at Nullagine, Mosquito Creek, etc.., are very rare.

2.   **Quartz reefs** which contain gold are almost invariably in greenstone country. Do not pass by a quartz reef in greenstone country, no matter what its colour. On the other hand, quartz reefs in granite country are frequently too poor, even with gold at present prices.

3.   **Lodes**. - Payahle lodes occur almost invariably in greenstone country, more particularly in those areas where the greenstone has been so sheared, foliated or schisted by pressure as to have lost the original massive structure. Payable lodes seldom occur and seldom persist in massive greenstone. The foliated portions of greenstone areas usually occur near to the junction with the massive granites. When prospecting for lodes keep within a mile or so of the contact of greenstone and granite. At the very least, let this narrow strip of country he the first prospected; and the next, where there is evidence of foliated and sheared. greenstone.

In jasper bar country, the jasper bars frequently occur relatively close to the granite contacts, and usually run parallel with them. Faults in the "bars" should he sought. It is often in faults or faulted zones that secondary enrichments occur, indicated by specially rich ore. Good examples occur at Lennonville, Boogardie, and Bull- finch. Quartz veins occurring outside the jasper veins should he sought. There are numerous instances of this class of reef having been profitably worked in the Yilgarn Field, in the vicinity of jasper bars extending from Cheriton in the South to Currajong in the North, a distance of 90 miles.

Alluvial ground consists of practically all surface deposits, and the gold in it occurs loose and is recovered by dryhlowing. Surface indications show what places are worth trying, or a piece of gold may he specked.

If surface gold is found it may indicate shallow or deep alluvial. Sink in the most likely place, you may bottom on clay or cement. But do not let that stop you. Beneath two or three feet of clay pan may be more alluvial carrying payable gold. Examine bottom for leaders, and sink down to the settled country, which may contain the source of supply of the alluvial gold. A deep lead has more pipe-clay at bottom as a rule, and is usually found in flats between two rising grounds or a rise on one side only, and is due to denudation and weathering freeing the gold from the lode and carrying it into deep or shallow gutters.

Lodes are altered country rock or fillings of cracks in them, and when they are mostly quartz are called "reefs." These occur along shear planes, and generally form an outcrop above the surrounding country. Where the lode matter is soft there will be no outcrop, and the lode may be covered up with surface material, but there will be pieces of rock or lode material somewhere about and near the covered-up lode, and it is these the prospector wants to look for -indications- and by dollying pieces of rock he may trace their source. Another method is by loaming above likely localities; loaming is filling the pan with earthy material and washing or dry-blowing it for colours. This method needs care and experience. Only when colours are got can it be of use.

There is often a local enrichment in the oxidised portions of lodes and reefs. Nevertheless, there are noted exceptions, e.g., Great Fingal, poor to 400 feet and the Meekatharra mines were all quartz leaders in the oxidised zone.

The prospector interested in the technical terms of his trade will find many of them in the Glossary immediately before the Index of this book.

The graphites are light-coloured and not favourable, though it is pretty certain the light-coloured rocks have had some influence in the occurrence of gold, as they are never far away from the rich lodes and reefs.

Always carry a few sample bags, and note where you get samples from. Use the dolly-pot all the time; it is the surest guide. Always clean out the pot with clean quartz after dollying a rich sample. If you want to test the sulphides roast the dollied ore on a piece of iron in the camp fire till red, and then pan off.

If you find a promising area peg it out, and apply for it within ten days and get an officer of the Department of Mines to have a look at it.

When panning off samples, particularly lode material, use clean water where possible. Thick, muddy water, or greasy water, tends to keep the fine gold afloat; thus, where high-grade ore has been previously panned off, the following samples might easily be "salted " by getting colours from the muddy water.

When prospecting quartz or lode material that has been shed from an ore body, gather a general sample of the loose material. Do not confine your attention to what you consider the likely looking stone, as it sometimes turns out that it is the unlikely looking material that carries the values. Having taken the general sample, break a portion of each stone or lode fragment, retaining the other portion. Dolly the general sample, and if gold is present the source can be found by a process of elimination. Try each retained piece separately.

Sometimes quartz outcrops to the surface mixed up
with other oxidised formations, and associated with mineral. This is a sign there may be sulphide ore underneath. In these circumstances sink through to sulphide, then cross-cut to adjacent strata, which may form a schist foot or hanging wall. Along these shear zones values are often found.

Standing off the shaft so as to intersect the ore body at a given depth may prove unfortunate. The ore may be impoverished where you intersect, and even laterally where you drive. Good values may exist immediately above the point of intersection. The shaft should be sunk on the ore body so that, while developing your mine, you are also prospecting it; and if the ore happens to be of payable grade, you are earning revenue at once. These are the advantages of sinking in the ore body.

A grab sample can be taken from the broken ore as it is pulled to the surface. A small portion is take from each bucket. This can then be dealt with on the lines set out in the article" Notes on the Taking and Preparation of Samples for Assay."

DRY-BLOWING

A well-known dictionary describes dry-blowing as "a method adopted in Western Australia for freeing pounded gold ore from the powdered matter when water is not available. It consists in slowly pouring the crushed material from one dish to another, and blowing away the powder with the mouth, as it falls, when there is not wind enough to do the work." Probably, the two dishes led to the "shaker", and that to the dry-blower.

The "shake" apparatus consists of a vertical series of sieves arranged in a light portable frame. The coarsest sieve (sheet iron, with punched holes) is at the top and rejects the largest fragments. What passes through to the second sieve contains all the fines, but there is still some coarse stuff for the second sieve to reject. There are two or three sieves. The frame is made of springy material, laths or bush sticks, and is usually home-made, but not always. The frame is given a rocking motion and, as the fines pass from sieve to sieve, the wind blows away the light dusty particles. The remainder under the last sieve is a concentrate that should contain all the values. It is still necessary to pour from dish to dish from an elevation (two or three feet) to permit the wind to get rid of the bulk of the dust. The final concentration is made with water and a panning-off dish.

The actual Dry-blowing machine is a more elaborate shaker, with a bellows that blows up through the sieves, and makes the operation more independent of the help of the wind.

LOAMING

Outcrops at one time occurred in profusion, but the sharp tooth of time has eaten most of them away. Weathering, Disintegrating, and Shedding are the three last stages in the history of outcrops. Gold is set free, and survives, either in that place, or further down the hill. Gold being six times heavier than ordinary rock, is more difficult to move, and will settle into rifts and hollows, perhaps in what is a watercourse in a wet season. When the prospector comes on the scene there is a cover of soil. He tests the watercourse and finds traces up to a certain point. From here he works up the hill, testing the soil systematically. When this "loaming" ceases to yield traces of gold, or when there is a marked diminution, it is time to put in a costean. A great deal of labour may he saved by using an auger for lateral prospecting. Shallow pits are sunk on the line of the proposed costean, and the intervening ground is bored by an auger with a jointed stem made of water pipe. An auger capable of boring twelve feet, can readily be carried, and in this case the pits could be twenty feet apart. By panning off the borings the ground can be thoroughly prospected. Note, however, that it may pay to continue still further up the hill, not only to the point where the signs of gold perceptibly fall. There may be a lower grade leader or lode higher up the slope. One of the most important functions in modern prospecting, especially in this State, is to locate large low grade deposits. Consider the results of investigations into Tindals, Big Bell, Wiluna, etc. Rich shoots are, of course, valuable to the prospector: they make it possible for him to continue, but he should keep the other possibility in mind. The "loam" should be got from shallow pits, not from the actual surface as a rule. Loaming is an important branch of prospecting methods. Gold-bearing bodies of a soft friable nature give, in a lot of cases, no indication whatever, as far as the eye can see on the surface. They have been weathered down to a level of the surrounding country rock. This is where loaming comes to the front. It can be done either with two dishes in a dry-blowing way, with a dry-blower itself, or by panning off with water. The last is by far the most satisfactory, if water is at hand. The method calls for a lot of patience and systematic application, and if the prospector is not prepared to devote time and brains to the job, he has little chance of success. The value of a reef or lode is never consistent throughout, and knapping or sampling of outcrops leave too much to chance. In a reef 24 inches wide, 22 inches of that width may he quite barren, and it is possible for the remaining two inches to be sufficiently rich to make the value of the whole reef, when hulked, highly payable. One seldom hears of a reef whose values are consistent throughout. Having this feature in view you must first dig a trench right across the reef, deep enough to disclose its undisturbed sectional formation, and then carefully sample each leaf or section separately. Another method is to take a portion of each separate make of stone in your sample.

The Dolly-pot is essential in gold prospecting where rock samples have to he crushed for testing. An iron mercury bottle with the top cut off is very suitable. In emergency a short length of pipe placed loosely on a plate of iron may answer. Even a jam or fruit tin placed on something solid can he made to do. In dollying it is very important that the same weight of ore should he taken each time. The pot should he free from particles of rich ore left over from previous samples. The only way to ensure this is to grind in the pot a little barren rock or quartz,

PROSPECTOR'S DISH

The Gold-washing Dish, or Pan, is the simplest of gold-saving appliances, but on account of its limited capacity is more used for testing purposes than for actual recovery of gold. Any utensil used for gold-washing must be free from grease or oil. Fine particles of gold contaminated with grease may float off and be lost. Occasionally turn the dish upside down over a small fire to remove casual grease, and when not in actual use always turn the dish upside down to avoid deposits of rust and fine material.

DISPOSAL OF BULLION

In districts where there are banking facilities it is usual for the gold producer to deal with one of the local hanks, and the bank will then make all necessary arrangements for the realisation of the bullion.

It is not necessary for such gold as hammered nuggets or alluvial to he melted into an ingot, Where there are no banking facilities, prospectors and others can deal direct with the Mint.

Gold may be sent through the post, but must be registered.

Gold posted should be well secured and the sender's name and address should be inside the parcel. Alluvial gold or small melted pieces may be packed in a paper or calico bag and placed in a round air-tight tobacco tin or similar container. Then the tin should be sewn in stout calico or canvas, and plainly addressed.

The parcel must be sent registered according to Post Office Regulations.

Where an owner of a battery or treatment plant has treated ore for a customer, the Mint can be asked to send the proceeds in two amounts, one to the owner of the battery for the charges, and one to the owner of the ore for the balance.

Any such request should be signed both by the battery owner and the prospector. Forms are available on request

GOLD MAY CONTAIN BASE METAL

The prospector may have copper in his ore, and the recovery method may give him copper as well as gold. Perhaps he does not recognise the coppery hue, and when his returns come in he is disappointed. Bullion that contains gold and a little silver should come bright from the mould. When copper and silver are present together in certain quantities, it is difficult to distinguish their presence merely by reference to colour. If it comes dull or black, then there is base metal content-zinc or bismuth or much copper, etc. Once the base metal has got into the ingot, better allow it to remain. Let the Mint do the refining. There are conditions, indeed, where it is not economical to produce high quality bullion. The object is to catch all the gold, and sometimes zinc or lead is caught at the same time.

The various warnings and admonitions about base metal may cause some misgiving about what the Mint is prepared to receive. To any who have doubts on this subject, it may be mentioned that the Mint has never objected to the form or quality of any gold received from the fields. But it is usually advantageous to the depositor to produce clean bullion. Many people think if an ingot contains gold, that the ingot is pure gold. All gold produced in W.A. contains some silver, and by the method of extraction there is at times an addition of copper, zinc, etc. Base metals should be kept out if possible, but it is not always economical to do so.

IS A TREATMENT PLANT JUSTIFIED

When gold ore has been found the question of a treatment plant arises, whether to install a battery (with amalgamating plates or strakes) and perhaps a cyanidation plant to treat the sands, or to cart to a State or privately owned battery.

LIMITS OF THE SMALL TREATMENT PLANT

In many cases grinding through a 900-mesh screen is sufficient to yield a good extraction by amalgamation and cyanidation, but where the gold is evenly distributed through the ore finer grinding may be necessary. In this case it may be better to classify the discharge from the battery into sand and slime, and to regrind the sand in a tube mill, ball mill or grinding pan. If at this point there seems to be a call for a Slimes Plant, it will appear we are going beyond the limits of a small show and the operators will have to be content with normal battery crushing and amalgamation, followed by leaching of the sand (or mixed sand and slime) with cyanide solution.

AMALGAMATION

Some ore may be more suitable for amalgamation than for cyanide treatment. Coarse gold, provided it has a clean surface, will readily respond to amalgamation. Finely divided gold dissolves rapidly in cyanide solution.

The owner should ask himself the following questions before installing a treatment plant :-

(1) Shall I be able to treat the ore more cheaply at my own plant than I could do at the nearest privately-owned crushing plant, es- pecially when taking into consideration the Cartage Subsidies allowable by the Government?

(2) Have I sufficient water? 350-500 gallons per ton is required.

(3) Is there sufficient firewood within a reasonable distance available to run a Gas Producer plant, if not, what will Fuel Oil cost landed at the mine?

(4) Can I raise sufficient capital to erect a plant estimated to cost £2,500 per stamp ?

When the owner has considered these questions, he must remember that some skilled labour is required to run any mechanical contrivance, especially in remote places, and that this labour is difficult to obtain unless the usual amenities are available.

He must also realise that if he and his partners propose to work the crushing plant themselves, as well as the Mine, both mine and the plant can only work part-time, resulting in lower production and higher costs per ton. Small treatment plants cannot he expected to treat ore at a low cost.

Large tonnage is essential for cheap mining and treatment. Private capital is generally available for the exploitation of shows producing large tonnages, and the owner of a small proposition should obtain the advice of an experienced mining man before incurring the expenses of erection and taking on the responsibility of running a crushing plant.

Many of the newly-found ore bodies consist of soft lode material which is easily crushed and the owner might consider the installation of a Huntingdon Mill, unless the ore is likely to get hard below water level.

A Stamp Mill will deal with any class of ore and crush in one stage from 2½-inch to 1600 mesh.

The finer the screen, the greater the liberation of finely divided gold; the slower the rate of crushing, the higher the cost of treatment.

The usual screens used are 800 and 900 mesh (i.e., the number of holes to the square inch), and made from 28 to 30 gauge wire. The gauge of the wire affects the size of the holes.

If there is sufficient ore, the question of installing a rock-crusher, elevator and bin can be considered.

A twelve-inch by eight-inch crusher and elevator, which will require an extra fifteen horsepower, will save the cost of a man on two shifts a day. Will the saving in wages outweigh the cost of interest, depreciation, and repairs to the extra plant?

In isolated centres distant from foundries and Engineering Works, over-mechanisation is not desirable, but some kind of self-feeder is desirable whether fed by hand or automatically.

As a rule, the cost of mining (that is, of sinking, breaking out the ore, and hauling it to the surface) is far greater than the cost of treating the ore.

It is therefore reasonable to say that a treatment plant should not be erected without counting the advantages and disadvantages.

Rather is it better to consider whether the money could be more profitably spent on improving the mining facilities.

A small Diesel-driven compressor with friction hoist for the ore, and a suitable pump for the water (if the mine is wet), could be installed at a quarter the cost of a five-stamp mill.

At first it may seem natural that the addition of a five-stamp mill will improve the property, but treatment plants need special experience and require extra labour. It may be preferable to mechanise the mine and thus push on its development.

In either case the question of a prime mover crops up. It may be run by steam, or Diesel, or producer gas. Usually the choice is between Diesel and Producer Gas. If there is sufficient firewood in the vicinity it is likely that producer gas will have the advantage. Otherwise enquiry should be made as to the cost of fuel oil delivered.

As a measure of assistance to those who have to transport their ore by road or rail to a State Battery or to a privately-owned battery, the Govern-

Government of Western Australia has granted a Cartage Subsidy. There is a form for making the claims and, when this is filled in, it may be handed to the Battery Manager. With the Manager's certificate it is forwarded to the Superintendent of State Batteries. The scale of the subsidy refers to all ore transported and is as follows:-

(1)	On ore carted by road, the subsidy shall be 9d. per ton per mile, less 1/6 per dwt. of bullion recovered per ton by amalgamation, calculated to the nearest half-dwt., with a minimum deduction of 6/- per ton and a maximum subsidy of 12/6 per ton.

(2)	When carted by road and rail, the subsidy shall be 9d. per ton per mile carted by road, plus railage, less a deduction of 1/6 per dwt. of bullion per ton recovered by amalgamation, with a minimum deduction of 6/- per ton and a maxi- mum subsidy of 12/6 per ton.

(3)	Payment of subsidy shall be restricted to ore received and raised by the present holders of mining tenements. Filling from old stopes or ore from the cleaning out of shafts shall not qualify for subsidies.

THE STAMP BATTERY

In D. Jacobsson's "Free State and New Rand Gold," he makes the following references to the Stamp Mill. "The Stamp Mill has become a crushing unit solely, its function nowadays being to reduce the rock sufficiently in size to be subsequently ground in the ball mills. Because this function can be achieved at less cost by crushers of the gyratory type, no new reduction plants erected on the Rand since 1918 have incorporated stamps at all. Yet clearly it would not be economic to scrap stamp mills already installed in favour of completely modern processes. The largest mill on the Rand (at Randfontein) has as many as 600 stamps under one roof." In Western Australia at the Sons of Gwalia and the Hannans North, the Stamp Mill is used as an intermediary between the Rock Breaker and the Ball Mill. At the Lake View, Squires Crushers are used as the intermediary.

Having arrived at the conclusion that there is enough payable ore to justify the erection of a five-stamp battery that will handle 100 tons of ore a week, and the necessary water supply being assured, some of the details can he discussed.

The stamp battery is not modern, in some respects it is not efficient, but it has the peculiar and often indispensable merit that it can crush any class of ore. It is essentially a pioneering machine, simple and rugged in design, all parts being replacable, and the few repairs likely to he required not beyond the resources of an outback mining field.

The choice of a suitable site is restricted by the necessity of its being near the show, not necessarily nearer the water supply, as water can be pumped more cheaply than ore can he carted.

Get a plan drawn by a competent man of the general layout. This is essential.

If possible, go down to solid rock for your battery and engine foundations. Do not put the plant on the hanging wall of any workings. Very serious failures can result from weak or unsuitable foundations.

Concrete foundations for the mill must he re-inforced. If the ore is very soft, wooden piles are preferable.

The amount of water fed to the mortar box must not be regulated by the water requirements of the plate. Extra water if required to supplement that coming from the box can be given to the plate by hose.

The crushed ore is discharged from the battery box by being splashed violently against the screen, and the splash is controlled by the number of drops per minute, the weight of the stamps, and the distance through which the stamp falls before it hits the mixture of ground ore and water in the box.

This mixture can be likened to a puddle, and the stamp to a stone cast by a small boy in order to splash as much mud, not water, out of the puddle.

If the mud in the puddle has just sufficient water mixed with .it to splash freely, and is kept violently agitated to keep the finely divided particles in suspension, more mud will be ejected from the puddle in each splash. The puddle in the box should be just sufficiently deep to form a rich splashable mixture of ground ore and water, and this depth in practice is approximately 2½ inches, and is called the depth of discharge; i.e., the vertical distance between the top of the dies and the bottom of the screen.

If the discharge is too deep, the vertical drop to the pulp level is shortened and the force of the splash lessened, and there is a tendency for the ore to build up on the dies with a consequent decrease in effective crushing.

To set a battery for crushing, see that the dies are set as level as possible in the box on dry sand or headings. The usual order of drop is 1, 3,

5, 2, 4 or 1, 4, 2, 5, 3. It is dangerous to allow adjacent stamps to drop consecutively.

Fix on the drop you require, and if the bottom of the tappets are all level, the bottoms of the shoes while hanging in the battery box should also he level, and this will ensure that each stamp has exactly the same distance to fall before it strikes the puddle. This is important as a difference of even half an inch in one stamp, will upset the rhythm of the mill and will result in a loss of efficiency.

The amount of water fed to the battery box is important. If too little, the crushed material is too dry to splash ; if too much, the splash in the box is not sufficient to eject it all, and the water level creeps up the screen and the splash is decreased. As soon as this is noticed the water should he curtailed.

"Keep the stamps on the bottom," is a saying which is not taken literally, hut means that as little material as possible should be under the stamp when it falls. The nearer the iron is to iron, the faster the crushing. A competent battery hand easily ascertains the oorrect amount by feeling the stamp, and sets his feeder accordingly.

The longer the drop, and the more often the stamps fall, the greater the crushing capacity of the battery.

The number of blows has a greater influence than the height of drop, but one is dependent on the other, because if the Mill runs too fast, the cam will catch the tappet before the stamp is on the bottom.

For hard ores, a seven-inch drop and 108 blows to the minute is about the maximum effective combination, but if the man in charge is not experienced, reduce the speed to 100.

For soft ores, the drop should be reduced, but only sufficient to keep the stamps off the bottom.

The pulp (pulverised ore) is passed over the plate with a flow of water sufficient to prevent the deposition thereon of undesirable material. As the mercury takes up gold it hardens and when the amalgam cannot be depressed with the ball of the finger, or when gold appears in the tailings, a clean up is necessary.

Usually the plates require dressing at least once a shift. Hang up the stamps, wash all sand off the plates and scrape the amalgam using a one per cent. solution of salammoniac, wash with water and rub in more mercury.

Amalgamation may be carried on in the mortar box and is regarded as good practice on many plants. With some ore it may not be successful, for instance, the presence of some sulphides may lead to flouring of the mercury.

BATTERY HINTS

Good solid foundations save endless trouble.

Don't neglect holding down bolt

Keep the stamps running at a regul

Keep gnides in good order, too much wear allows stamps to strike one another and knock heads off.

Broken stems should he heated to redness to remove crystallisation (fatigue).

A good set of keys for tappets and pulleys soon pays for itself.

Learn how to lubricate bearings and working parts. Wasteful or bad lubrication is costly, and makes a horrid mess. Watch the loose pulleys.

Keep belts well dressed with castor oil, supple belts and burnished pulleys do good work. Hard belts slip.

Keep an eye on the packing in glands, it doesn't last for ever.

Leaky glands and joints lead to stoppages and costly

repairs.

Don't wait for tanks, vats, etc., to rust, protect them with tar or paint.

Maintenance is a golden rule, a stitch in time saves money.

There should be a place for every tool, and every tool

should he in its place. See you don't forget it.

The height of discharge in a battery box is important, try a 2½-inch discharge.

PREPARATION AND CARE OF BATTERY PLATES

For the amalgamating plates soft, rolled copper plate of one-eighth inch should be used, providing an average surface of two square feet per ton of ore treated each 24 hours.

New plates should get the following treatment:-

(1) Scour surface with fine sand, using a piece of bagging wrapped round a block of wood. (2) Wash with strong solution of soda ash. (3) Wash with a one per cent. solution of soda ash. (4) Wash with clean water. (5) Have

a mixture of fine sand with salammoniac and a little mercury. With a clean stiff scrubbing brush, scrub this mixture into the plate till it is coloured with mercury. (6) Let the plate stand 24 hours, then scrub mercury into it till it can absorb no more. (7) If possible give a coat of silver amalgam, using a cloth wetted with a solution of salammoniac: four ounces to a pint of water. It is essential that the amalgamated plate be kept in a bright condition. If it becomes discoloured there will be losses of gold. It may be necessary to keep swabbing new plates with cyanide solution while in use, until a good coating of amalgam is secured. Grease rapidly causes sickening of mercury, and must not be allowed to come in contact with the plates.

Sufficient water is necessary to keep the copper plates free from sand lodgment There is no advantage in using too much water, and it costs money to supply it.

Too much mercury in the boxes will make the copper plates "sloppy." The amalgam caught on copper plates should he firm but soft, too much mercury makes it soft enough for globules to run down the plate, causing loss. Too little mercury makes the amalgam hard and brittle. Keep the happy medium and get good amalgamation.

Some minerals make the plates dirty. In such cases wipe them over with a cloth now and again, but don't get fussy about it.

Keep grease away from battery plates. Don't wipe them with oily rags or waste.

SICKENING OF MERCURY

A term used to describe its condition when coated with thin films of base-metal compounds derived from the ore, or from impurities in the mercury itself-may cause much trouble. Arsenic, antimony, and bismuth are the worst promoters of sickening and cause a black film to coat the mercury so that it will not amalgamate gold nor coalesce. Grease, graphite, talc and clay and similar materials cause a form of sickening by protectively covering the mercury surface and inducing mechanical separation; they also cause a loss by coating of the gold particles. Most base-metal sulphide minerals will sicken mercury if partly oxidised. The oxidisation of sulphide minerals that form acid in the water is often counteracted by adding lime to the ore feed. The use of some sodium amalgam on the plates increases recovery from some troublesome ores, as it is a powerful amalgamator and will take up many substances that cause sickening, although it does not help very much on antimonial ores. Where sickening is particularly active, occasional cleaning with weak cyanide or other solution is advisable to remove the impurities and brighten the plates. - *United States Bureau of Mines*

CLEAN-UP OF MORTAR BOX

The "headings" or contents of the mortar box consisting of pulp, gravel, minerals, pieces of iron and steel and mercury, are either panned off by hand or washed in a sluice box or over the copper plates. Those portions of the headings containing gold are collected and placed in a bucket or bowl of mercury and well stirred. The dross will float and the gold will sink. The surface should be carefully skimmed. The skimmings should then be mag- neted to remove the iron and steel, and the magnetings should be set aside until they rust thoroughly (perhaps a month or two) when they can be ground in a mortar. Any specks of gold amalgam will be liberated and can be recovered in mercury, the final skimmings being discarded. The skimmings, which have been magneted, should be thoroughly ground in a mortar by hand or in a suitable pan with a little mercury, with the continual addition of water to wash off the valueless dirt. They should then he placed in the bucket or bowl of mercury and well stirred. This process should he repeated once or twice, and the final skimmings set aside. They, like the discarded magnetings, may contain a little gold only recoverable by a smelting works or mint.

CLEAN-UP OF PLATES

The plates should be washed with clean water, and the amalgam removed with blunt scrapers. The plates should then be washed down, and all loose amalgam col- lected. The plates should then be sprinkled with mercury and rubbed with a little fine sand and a piece of bag or soft wood to loosen any remaining amalgam. After wash• ing again the plates should be rubbed down with pieces of hard rubber to remove all amalgam. The rubbing down with mercury and sand can be repeated if necessary.

COLLECTING THE AMALGAM

When the amalgam from the plates has all been collected it should be placed in the bucket or bowl of mercury, and be well stirred. Any copper or other dross from the plates will float, and should be carefully skimmed off. Floating particles of iron or steel can be removed with a hand magnet. These skimmings should be treated with those from mortar box.

The gold amalgam will be found in the bottom of the qcket or bowl, and the whole should now be well stirred again to get rid of any remaining dross, which should be carefully skimmed off. The mercury should then be squeezed in chamois leather or suitable canvas, when the gold amalgam will be recovered in the shape of quite hard balls. The squeezed amalgam (and the mercury, if necessary) should be retorted in the usual way, and the mercury recovered.

RETORTING THE AMALGAM

The retort receives a wash of clay or. lime inside to prevent sticking. Then the balls of mercury are placed inside perhaps each wrapped in paper. Close, seal and keep at a low temperature until most of the mercury has distilled off.

When any holder of a mining tenement decides to abandon his holding it is obligatory upon him to lodge a surrender of his title. with Mercury leaves the amalgam as vapour and the cooling system has to be good to reduce the vapour to liquid.

But there will be some vapour and it is poisonous. The work should be done in a current of air, better still in the open.

As the retorting is finishing the temperature will be slightly raised. The retort can then be removed from the fire to cool. On becoming cool enough to handle the retort can be opened and the retorted gold taken out.

The retorted gold can be smelted in a graphite crucible with a little borax glass, poured into a mould, and be allowed to cool off. The bar of bullion can then be quenched in weak acid or water and, if the correct procedure has been adopted, should contain comparatively small amounts of base metal.

Skimmings or dross of any kind should not he melted with the retorted gold.

Skimmings and dross from the various operations in the treatment plant are likely to contain gold, hut they also include iron and zinc and perhaps copper and lead. It is no use keeping the amalgam free from such impurities if they are to he melted with the bullion.

A SIMPLE CYANIDE PLANT

Cyanide is a deadly poison and must he handled and used with extreme care.

The cheapest and most simple method of cyanidation is leaching. For this the following equipment is required:

I. *Dissolving Tank.* A small tank of wood or galvanised iron, dressed with tar, in which strong solutions are mixed before being run into the solution vat.

2. *Solution Vat.* A larger tank in which are held standard solutions.

3. *Leaching Vat.* Wood or galvanised iron tank tarred throughout and in which is placed a filter bottom. The filter bottom can be made by spacing brickbats about one inch apart. These are covered with hessian or hags, on which is placed a layer three inches thick of coarse sand. The sands to he treated are placed on top of this A vat twelve feet by three feet gives a handy-sized charge. The vat has pipe fittings, one to lead the cyanide solution into the vat ; the other to drain the solution, when gold-hearing, to the zinc box.

4. *Zinc or Extractor Boxes.* These are long and contain zinc shavings to precipitate the gold from the solution. The boxes have compartments, and the arrangement is designed to force the solution to contact as much zinc as possible.

5. *A Sump or Residue Tank* into which used solutions are stored before being sent through the plant again.

Vessels for the clean-up :-

6. Tub for washing zinc from boxes.

7. Dish to hold long zinc washed for re-use.

8. Drum or vat for aciding sludge from boxes.

9. Cask for storing sludge.

10. Cask for liquors from aciding drum.

CYANIDING

Some ores produce large percentages of slime and the tailing is difficult to leach and requires long treatment.

If the tailing is dried thoroughly before mixing and the surface of the content of the vat is never uncovered by solution 1:.11.; water until the final draining-a reasonable extraction can he got even on a tailing consisting of 60 per cent. slime and 40 per cent. sand.

To keep the surface covered use the ordinary ball tap used by squatters in their troughs. These taps can he fitted to the ordinary 1½ inch or 2-inch solution and water pipes with a reducing nipple and transferred from vat to vat as required.

If necessary the sandy part of the tailing can he segregated in a settler allowing the slime to overflow for sub- sequent treatment.

Don't attempt to cyanide in the settler, as the sand packs too hard for leaching and there is always a residue of wet slime in hands. It is therefore necessary to remove the settled sand to a vat for cyaniding.

OPERATING THE CYANIDE PLANT

A charge of dry sands is placed in (No. 3) the leaching vat, to within eighteen inches of the top. A solution of quicklime is allowed to percolate through the charge and then run off without going through the rest of the plant. Some sands do not require this treatment, but at times up to 2½ lb. lime per ton of sands may be necessary.

A cyanide solution is then made up and placed in the (No. 2) solution vat. Strength, 0.1 to 0.15 per cent. potassium cyanide, KCN.

After standing overnight the first cyanide solution charge is drawn off through the zinc box into (No. 5) the sump. From the sump the solution goes back to (No. 3) the leaching vat, and the next day it is run through the (No. 4) zinc box, and so on for several days. One ton of water is 224 gallons.

SAND AND SLIMES

Should sand and slimes have to be treated, it is necessary to have them dry. The mixture should be about half and half. Care must be taken not to pack this mixture, or it will he difficult to get the solution through it.

As the solution passes through the drain cock it may contain some slime. If this is the case, the first compartment of the zinc box can be used as a settler, and thus prevent the slime from fouling the zinc in the other compartments.

The solution entering the boxes should

(a)   contain a trace of free cyanide ;

(b)   he slightly alkaline ;

But if the ore contains iron pyrites or antimony, or if the water contains excess of magnesium, it may he better for the solution at this stage to he neutral, with any unavoidable variation slightly on the alkaline side.

If the precipitation is going on satisfactorily a gas (hydrogen) will he rising from the zinc, particularly in the first two compartments used on zinc, where the bulk of the gold is precipitated.

USE OF LEAD NITRATE OR LEAD ACETATE

For weak or coppery solutions the zinc shavings should be dipped in a lead salt until a black film comes on the zinc. The zinc shavings thus coated should be put in the boxes immediately and the compartments filled with solu- tion. (The coated shavings oxidise rapidly in the air.)

The lead salt may be used for the precipitation of soluble sulphides, but in this case it should be added in an intermediate filter or clarifier to enable the re-action to take place there and not in the boxes.

Avoid agitating the zinc boxes in the presence of air as freedom from oxygen favours gold precipitation.

NOTES ON HOW TO CLEAN UP A SMALL CYANIDE PLANT

It is assumed that the precipitation of gold from cyanide solutions has been effected by zinc shavings in an ordinary extractor box of several compartments.

Stop the flow of solution through the box, and siphon most of the solution out of each compartment. Then start to clean out the top compartment, Any long zinc useful for further precipitation should be well washed in a tub (No. 6) of clean water to remove any loose gold, and should be placed in a dish (No. 7) for re-use. All sludge (gold and fine 'zinc) in the first compartment should be transferred to a wooden tub (No. 6), the compartment being thoroughly cleaned out. Most of the gold will be found in the first compartment if the box has been properly attended to from day to day.

Then proceed with the second and subsequent compartments, washing all long zinc thoroughly and replace it in the dish (No. 7). Each compartment in its turn should be well cleaned, and all sludge should be transferred to the cask. When all compartments have been cleaned out and the long zinc placed in the upper compartments, new zinc is added as required to the lower compartments. When this is done the solutions can then be allowed to flow through the extractor box again.

The contents of the tub (No. 6) in which zinc has been washed are then transferred to the drum (No. 8) which should he filled with clean water, well stirred, and allowed to settle.

(When much copper is present in the sludge a roast may be given here, before the sulphuric acid treatment. The advantages are (1) the copper oxidises and is readily dissolved in the sulphuric, (2) the zinc is oxidised, and as zinc oxide dissolves in the acid more quietly, (3) avoidance of fumes from decomposition of cyanogen solutions, (4) cutting out use of nitric. In the hands of a careful operator, roasting gold sludge can be effected without loss of importance. The sludge should not be stirred when it is becoming dry, or gold will be lost by dusting. The method of making and using a roasting pan is given later.)

Into the drum (No. 8) pour some warm water. Pour into the water as much sulphuric acid as will make a ten per cent. solution. Half a kerosene tin of water to half a Winchester quart of sulphuric acid is about the right proportion.

Be very careful to pour the acid slowly and steadily to prevent splashing, as it can inflict a nasty burn.

When the contents of the (No. 6) tub have settled, siphon off and collect the clear liquor in a suitable tank or vessel for subsequent treatment. The sludge should then he added to the acid in handfuls at a time, stirring with a stick continuously. This should be done in the open air, in order that the fumes will blow away and do no harm. Do not add too much sludge to the acid at one time. It usually takes a couple of hours at least to complete aciding, hut will take much longer if sludge is added too quickly, or if acid is poured on to the sludge instead of as described. Keep stirring right through the process.

(If much copper is present in the sludge, and the roast treatment described above has not been given, add sufficient but small quantities of nitric acid, which will dissolve the copper.)

When the sulphuric acid has done its work, fill the (No. 8) drum with water, warm if available, stir well and allow to settle properly. Then siphon the clean liquor from the drum and collect it in the (No. 10) liquor cask. Fill the cask with clean fresh water, stir thoroughly, and allow to settle again. The second settling will be quicker than the first, and may take only half an hour or so, whilst the first settling may require an hour. Siphon off the clear liquor, and send it to (No. 10) liquor cask.

Then transfer the washed sludge to a filter made of double unbleached calico sewn to a hoop and in the form of an inverted cone or bag. When it has drained, gently pour on to it a gallon or two of hot to boiling water, and allow to drain. Then cut the calico from the hoop, and transfer the lot to a roasting pan. A roasting pan may be made from a sheet of black iron with the edges turned up, say, four or five inches, the corners crimped, not cut. A convenient size is five feet by two feet. To prevent it from buckling, place it on a sheet of fairly heavy iron or steel to keep the heat of roasting from direct contact with the pan. To it add a small amount of nitre (dis-solved in hot water), not more than 2½ per cent. of the weight of sludge. Apply heat gradually, stirring well while the sludge is moist. It will become rubbly before dry, but do not stir when it becomes dry, because gold will be lost by dusting. Bring it to a red heat, but do not overheat and fuse it. The calico will be burnt and be reduced to ash. Keep at a dull red heat for half an hour then allow to cool.

Transfer the roasted sludge to a crucible, add 50 per cent. by weight of borax glass and melt. If the sludge is not as clean as it should be, add with the borax glass a little bicarbonate of soda and sand. The slags from gold melting should be saved, with any dross or skimmings from amalgam.

The liquors siphoned off during the clean-up should he allowed to settle for a week, when the clear liquor should be run to waste and the residue in the tank should be cleaned out, dried and melted. The extractor box should he attended to daily or as often as necessary. Do not add new shavings to the top compartment, but move up shavings from the second compartment, and so on. All new shavings should he added to the bottom compartments. Avoid handling shavings with oily hands.

In cases where ores contain copper or other refractory materials, new zinc shavings should he dipped in a five per cent. solution of acetate of lead for a moment, or until they show a film of lead. On no account should a heavy coating of lead he allowed to precipitate on the zinc. It should then he drained and used in the usual way.

TESTING THE CYANIDE SOLUTION

When a solution of Silver Nitrate is added to a solution of Potassium Cyanide, a white precipitate of Silver Cyanide is formed and immediately dissolved by any free Potassium Cyanide present. On the completion of the reaction, however, there no longer being any free Potassium Cyanide left in the solution, the white precipitate ceases to dissolve.

The test consists of taking a measured quantity of the Potassium Cyanide solution, and cautiously adding Silver Nitrate solution of known strength, a few drops at a time, until a precipitate forms which does not re-dissolve.

The strength of the Potassium Cyanide can then he estimated from the amount of Silver Nitrate solution used.

REQUIRED FOR THE ACTUAL TEST

1.   A bottle of standard Silver Nitrate solution such that 1 c.c. = 0. 005 gram of Potassium Cyanide. This is made by dissolving 6 .159 gram pure Silver Nitrate in distilled water and diluting with distilled water to one litre. This solution should never he exposed to direct sunlight.

2.   A burette for measuring Silver Nitrate solution only.

3.   A 50 c.c. graduated cylinder for measuring Cyanide solution only.

4.   A one per cent. solution of Potassium Iodide.

5.   A 350 c.c. beaker in which the test is made.

Using a Silver Nitrate solution of the above concen• tration and 50 c.c. of Cyanide solution for each deter- mination, each c.c. of Silver Nitrate solution used in the determination represents O. 01 per cent. KCN potassium cyanide.

METHOD OF THE TEST

Measure out exactly 50 c.c. of Cyanide solution into the beaker, add 5 c.c. of Potassium Iodide solution, and add Silver Nitrate solution from the hurette, a few drops at a time, shaking well. Continue until the solution is permanently cloudy. Divide the number of c.c. of Silver Nitrate solution used by 100 to obtain the percentage of free Potassium Cyanide.

PROTECTIVE ALKALINITY

The determination of protective alkalinity is also important and may he made on the same solution as is used for free Cyanide determination. For this determination the following additional solutions are required :-

1.   Oxalic Acid solution containing 11.25 gram crystallised Oxalic Acid in one litre of distilled water.

2.   Phenoiphthalein solution made by dissolving 0.5 gram of Phenolphthalein in 100 c.c. of Methylated Spirit.

METHOD OF THE TEST

After determining the free Cyanide, run in a little more Silver Nitrate solution, add one drop of Phenolphthalein solution and run in the Oxalic Acid solution from a burette until the pink colour is discharged and the solution again becomes yellow. Divide the number of c.c. of Oxalic Acid solution used by 100 to obtain the percentage of lime, CaO, in the Cyanide solution.

        (A second burette is required, to be used solely for Oxalic Acid solution.)

PEGGING-OUT A TAILINGS DUMP

Tailings that have reverted to the rown may be acquired to remove or treat.

An application for a licence to remove or treat tailings or other mining material under Section 112 (Mining Act) shall be made to the Warden or Mining Registrar. The applicant shall at the time of making the application post up a notice thereof at the Warden's Office and on the heap of tailings to be removed or treated and shall forthwith advertise the notice in a local newspaper.

The notice should state the estimated tonnage of the heap, the number of the cancelled tenement upon which the heap lies, and the period for which the licence is applied for, which period must not exceed twelve months. The notice should be attached to a peg not less than three feet high and should be placed in a prominent position on the heap. The time and date of taking possession should also show on the notice. The fee payable for a licence is 10/- per month, and the fee must be lodged with the application. Application forms are available at any Mining Registrar's Office.

CYANIDING DUMPS

It is important to examine the nature of the material before erecting a plant. A sand with low values may be more profitable than a mixture of sand and slime with greater gold content. The slimes may be present in sufficient amount to require filter presses or other additional plant. The cost of extra plant, etc.., may make the proposition unpayable. Before any decision, it is necessary to ascertain:-

    (1)   the gold assay per ton;

    (2)   the tonnage;

    (3)   how much can be extracted by cyanidation.

Even if the gold assay appears high, local conditions may make recovery unpayable. The tonnage may not be sufficient to justify the erection of a plant. If the material is refractory it may not lend itself to cyanide treatment.

On these points, to avoid unprofitable expense and disappointment, it is necessary to have expert judgment.

The cyanide process requires experience and should not be undertaken without some preliminary practical knowledge. It must be remembered that the solutions of cyanide and the gases from them are poisonous.

Prospectors engaged in milling or cyaniding, who meet with difficulties in the treatment of their ores, are advised to communicate with the Director, School of Mines, Kalgoorlie.

VALUING A DUMP

When it is proposed to acquire a Cyanide Residues Dump there are three questions which should be asked. What is its size? What is its average assay? What treatment will it require? Each of these questions is important. A dump which will respond to a simple treatment may be too small to interest a company, but big enough, to give wages to one man operating for himself A very much larger dump with a smaller assay may require elaborate plant, and still be a good proposition for a company with capital. But great size and comparative high assay will not serve if the treatment required is too expensive to yield a surplus.

SAMPLING A TAILINGS DUMP

Tailings dumps are usually sufficiently flat to permit of all sampling to be done by vertical bore holes. The boring can be done by an auger with a pointed stem made of water pipe. Divide the surface of the dump into a number of imaginary equal areas and obtain a representative sample from each such area, so as to give a distance of, say, 30 feet between each bore (see Fig. 1). The bore holes to he deep and preferably to the bottom of the dump. If vertical distribution of values is required, each bore can be sampled in sections, thus :-

Sample la   0 to 6 ft.

      lb   6 to 12 ft.

      lc   12 to 18 ft.

If the holes are approximately the same depth the average value can he obtained by simply adding up the assay value of individual holes, and dividing by the number of holes. If there is any considerable difference in the depth of the holes, the average value can he obtained by working out the product of the depth and the value for each hole, finding the sum of these "products" and dividing by the sum of the depths. See following form:

Bore	Depth	Value	" Depth × Value "
No. 1 ..	....	....	....
No. 2 ..	....	....	....
No. 3 ..	....	....	....
No. 4 ..	....	....	....
No. 5 ..	....	....	....
No. 6 ..	....	....	....
etc.			
	Sum of Depths		Sum of " depth × value "

$$\text{Average value} = \frac{\text{Sum of " depth } \times \text{ value "}}{\text{Sum of depths}}$$

The outer or top two feet of the borings should not be included in the sample.

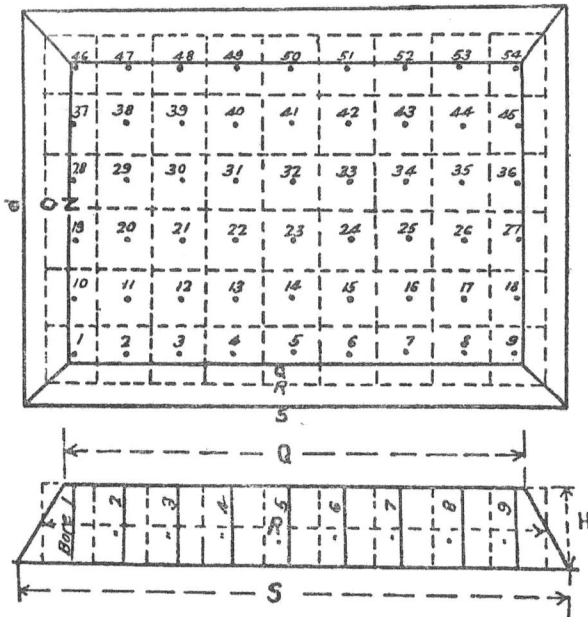

Fig. 1.

TAILINGS DUMP

PLAN AND CROSS SECTION SHOWING METHOD OF SAMPLING
Note.-The Dump is divided into a number of imaginary equal areas, in the centre of each of which a bore is put down through the Dump.

MEASURING A TAILINGS DUMP

If the dump is of a fairly regular pyramidal shape, then the formula is :-

Add the area of the top, the area of the bottom, and four times the area midway. Divide the sum by six, and multiply the result by the vertical height. If the measure- ments have been in feet, then the result is the volume in cubic feet. A cuhic foot of quartz, pulverised, and well packed, weighs about one hundredweight - greenstone about 1½ cwt.

Measurements should be carefully made.

The vertical height is required, not the length along the slope. The other measurements required are width along the top (N), midway (0) and bottom (P), and length along the top (Q), midway (R), and bottom (S). See Fig. 1.

When the shape of the dump is irregular, judgment is required in conforming the measurements to give an approximation of the diagram.

ANOTHER METHOD OF MEASURING

The particulars of depths given by the method of sampling on a previous page may be used for measuring the dump. Assuming that the bores are at 30 feet itervals, and are taken in each case to the bottom of the dump, then the expression - 30 x 30 x the sum of the depths in feet - gives the content of the dump in cubic feet. This method is appropriate when the tailings have been run into the bed of a creek, or upon very irregular or sloping ground.

WEIGHT OF A CUBIC FOOT

The weight of a cubic foot of the dump can best be ascertained by making an excavation 12 in. x 12 in. x 12 in., and weighing the amount of tailings excavated after drying it carefully.

CYANIDE DUMPS

Sampling cyanide tailings has its difficulties. When a tailings dump has existed for some time there may be an enrichment of the outer surface. In certain conditions moisture with gold in solution tends by gravity or capillary attraction to seek the surface. Once there it evaporates, leaving a deposit of gold. Thus to make a " grab sample" by taking a handful here and there from the surface, is quite unsuitable. Decomposing pyrite in a dump ie a serious cause of trouble.

Dumps may he considered under four headings :-
1.   Sand dumps, untreated by cyanide.
2.   Sand dumps, treated by cyanide.
3.   Slime dumps, untreated by cyanide.
4.   Slime dumps, treated by cyanide.

I do not think (writes a friend) that any true sand dump is enriched at the surface by capillarity certainly, not an untreated sand dump. But all sand dumps are enriched at the surface by wind concentration of gold particles, or gold-bearing mineral particles. Genuine slime dumps, untreated by cyanide, are in my opinion never concentrated at the surface. Dumps which are partly slime and partly sand may he enriched at the surface, hut it depends on the percentage of sand and mineral concentrate. Slime dumps which have been treated by cyanide are very dangerous to the sampler, because concentration at the surface is almost a certainty.

POST DIGGERS v. AUGERS .

Augers are in common use for sampling (we are advised) but they are not a patch on a post-hole digger for getting a true sample. With a three-inch post-hole digger you can go down 30 feet, and see the bottom with a sun reflection from a looking glass, in any ordinary dump. It is seldom that you can do this with an auger, as the top material is always falling down when using an auger.

NOTES ON THE TAKING AND PREPARATION OF SAMPLES FOR ASSAY

(It is said that good samplers are rare. Without instruction few men would realise that there is an unconscious impulse to make the sample as rich as possible. This is a sort of self-deception like cheating at "Patience." The good sampler treads a narrow path, rejecting all sentiment, following a strict rule that is in its way a sort of piety.)

One piece of stone is a specimen, not a sample. A specimen shows the mineral character of a rock or ore, whereas a sample is intended to show its value and must represent a heap of ore or a lode at some particular place. But a specimen stone is of value and should accompany the sample, hut not in the same bag.

To enable a correct estimate of the value of an ore to he made, a sample must he representative; or in other words, it is a small quantity of the original mass which contains, in the same proportion, all the constituents of the original mass. A single sample may not give accurately the value of a lode, hut the average of a number of samples should give a value differing very little from that of the body of ore which they represent. Therefore, in determining the value of a body of ore, more accurate results will he obtained by taking the average of a number of samples than by depending on a single sample.

In sampling a lode, samples should he taken at regular intervals, and the lode should he sampled over measured widths at right angles to the lode, i.e., along the shortest distance between the walls. The sample should he taken as evenly as possible over the whole width, and all the material broken should he included in the hulk sample. The hulk sample should then he broken into smaller pieces, well mixed, and quartered down. This consists in piling the ore into a cone on a floor, flattening out the cone, and dividing the heap into four equal parts by two cuts at right angles to each other. Two opposite quarters are taken for the sample, the other two being discarded. By successive finer crushing and quartering, the size of the sample is finally reduced to one or two pounds, which will accurately represent the original hulk sample. This constitutes the assay sample, which should he forwarded, preferably with a larger specimen of the ore, for inspection. Between successive quarterings the size of the pieces should he reduced by at least one half to ensure uniform mixing of the valuable material.

A pile of broken ore may be sampled by quartering, or by taking as a sample one shovelful out of each definite number of shovelfuls.

Samples for assay should always he dried, preferably in the sun, not over a fire, as overheating may cause alterations in the nature of the ore, especially in the case of sulphide ores, where oxidation of the sulphide minerals will take place if the ore is heated too strongly.

FREE ASSAYS

The following are the main conditions under which Free Assays are made at the Government Chemical Laboratories, Perth, and at the School of Mines, Kalgoorlie, for bona fide prospectors :-

The sample must have been obtained within the State, from land not held under lease for mining purposes.

The exact locality where the sample was found must he disclosed.

The sample must he of sufficient promise to warrant an assay being made at the expense of the State.

Free assays will not be made of samples showing free gold, or of tailings or other metallurgical products, or of umpire samples.

Prospectors who intend to treat their own ore or cyanide tailings may have laboratory tests made at the School of Mines, Kalgoorlie, to determine the most suitable method of treatment and the extraction that may he expected. Applications for this form of assistance, for which a fee is charged, should he made to the Director, School of Mines, Kalgoorlie. Those who are actively engaged in milling and cyaniding will also he assisted in overcoming difficulties met with in the treatment of their ore.

PICKS AND DRILLS

As an experienced prospector remarks, it is most important that miners should use sharp picks and drills. Sometimes prospectors use picks or drills which have quite lost their sharpness. In such a case the output is low enough to lead to discouragement. Our adviser has a supply of picks and on a suitable day he proceeds to shape and temper all points that require attention. His forge is a bucket and his anvil a large hammer. Railway iron would serve. A petrol bucket perforated for the free play of air as used for cooking will do very well. Then the bucket is filled with roots or other good fuel, supported four inches above the surface of some high place, say, the dump. The high position is necessary to get the full benefit of the wind. This would not he enough, however, if a windy day were not chosen. Presently there will be a mass of glowing charcoal. Into this the pick points are to be inserted, about three or four inches. The opening in the bucket through which the pick points are inserted should face the wind. This will be probably enough to protect the handles from scorching, but in any case the handles must be protected. When the pick point is a cherry red or past a dull red, it will be hot enough to forge. A fitter's hammer and some sort of anvil will be required. When this forging is finished there remains the tempering. Bring the point to a cherry red heat and quickly quench in water. A patch on the point must then be cleaned bright with a stone or perhaps an emery cloth to enable colours to be seen clearly. Hold point over fire and watch for colours that will appear-first the straws, then red-brown, followed by light blue. When light blue appears, plunge in water. This should give a hard but not brittle point. It is to be noted that the pick point is usually carbon steel welded on the body, which may be iron or mild steel. The welding on of a new point requires facilities and skill not usually available outback. However, some veteran prospectors can re-steel a pick with very little equipment. With certain changes which need not be described, the method for pick points is followed in sharpening and tempering drills.

TOOLSMITH'S CHART FOR CARBON STEEL TOOLS

Temper	Carbon %	Heating for Forging—Maximum Colours	Heating for Hardening—Maximum Colours	Tempering Colours	Purpose
1	1/2	Cherry Red	Cherry Red	Dark Straw	Lathe tool
2	1 1/2	Bright cherry red	do.	Light straw	do.
3	1 1/4	Red	do.	Straw	Taps, drills, punches
4	1	Full red	do.	Red brown	Large drills
5	7/8	Bright red	Bright cherry red	Light blue	Springs, chisels, smith's tools, prospecting drills
6	3/4	Full bright red	do.	Dark blue	Rivet snaps, etc.

All steels should be heated very slowly at first until the tools are evenly heated well through and should then be brought to the proper temperature as quickly as possible. Steel should not be allowed to soak in the fire.

EXPLOSIVES

GENERAL

Blasting explosives are substances which on firing change almost instantly into other forms, mainly gaseous, with development of heat, pressure and displacement or shock. The great volume of gases, expanded by high temperature, presses on the confining medium, which at the same time is stressed by the rapidly-moving explosion wave. These effects combine to shatter and dislodge whatever material is to be blasted. There is no truth in the old belief that explosives strike downward; actually the effect tends to spread in all directions. The misunderstanding arises from the common observation that when explosive is fired on a solid surface like rock or hard soil, breakage or cratering remains as evidence, but the surrounding air, though receiving the same impetus, shows no lasting effect from the disturbance.

COMPOSITION AND PROPERTIES OF EXPLOSIVES

New prospectors and others unfamiliar with explosives will naturally want to know something about the different grades, their purposes and how they may he obtained, transported, stored and prepared for use. Of the many varieties, less than a dozen usually covers the field in mining, whilst for prospecting two or three will generally suffice for the early stages. All except blasting powder are composed essentially of nitroglycerin, thickened or gelatinized with nitrocotton and incorporated with oxidising alients and other chemicals in proportions suited to given purposes, and to ensure complete explosion with a minimum of poisonous fume. Explosives labelled "Polar" are the same as ordinary grades except for inclusion of a substance to prevent freezing-a circumstance unlikely to occur with properly stored explosives in most parts of W.A. The pink or red tint often found is due to an anti-setting reagent which delays hardening, hut as the same purpose may be attained by colourless compounds, colour must be regarded as an incidental property having no hearing on the effectiveness of any particular explosive.

The same principle applies to safety fuse, once blue or grey hut now yellow for better contrast against dark-coloured rock. Most explosives are obtainable in different diameters, the one-inch being very widely used. Packaged in the well-known pine or fibreboard boxes, lined with moisture-resistant material, the plugs may either be loose or done up in ten five pound cardboard cartons, wrapped in waxed paper. The latter scheme is recommended for the small or casual user because a hulk- packed case on opening cannot readily be resealed to prevent access of moist air.

VARIETIES AND USE

A few varieties of explosive and their properties of interest to the prospector and small-show miner include: A.N. Gelatin Dynamite.- High strength, high density explosive suitable for all development work in the hardest rocks. Often preferred for winzing and shaft-sinking.

A.N. Gelignite 60.- High strength, high density. The most commonly used explosive in hard rock mining. Has good waterproofing qualities.

Semigel.- High strength, medium density explosive. When used in dry conditions, Semigel can replace a gelatinous explosive for stoping and development work in all but the hardest of rocks. In very hard rock, where full-round firing is 'practised, Semigel in the " burn-cut " holes often gives improved results.

Quarry Monobel.- A powder type of explosive of high strength, low density and no water resistance. Suitable for shooting the softer rocks. Ideal for burn-cut holes in drives and rises in hard rock. Neither this explosive nor Semigel would be particularly suitable in hard rock where the centre-cut type round is used.

Plastergel.- Designed for plaster-shooting (mud-capping or blistering) where the explosive is laid on the rock and covered with clay or mud. Would only be used for secondary blasting where it was not desirable to drill pop holes.

CONVEYANCE

Next comes the conveyance of explosives thus purchased to the point of use. Large amounts are railed, where practicable, or transported by road under permit, hut for the man concerned with only a few pounds or half-case, the interests of safety are best served by carrying the parcel in a wooden box covered with a tarpaulin as additional protection, and so placed on the vehicle as to be readily removable should fire or accident occur. Keep detonators, if possible, in the original cardboard-lined tin which may be stowed in glove box or similar position well away from the explosives. Safety fuse, having no mass explosion risk, need only he wrapped and put under cover from sparks, direct sunlight, moisture and grease.

STORAGE

The above suggestions apply in certain measure to methods of storage, and it must be borne in mind that a heavy responsibility rests on anyone to keep his explosives safely and securely. They should never be left about, even temporarily, because if falling into unauthorised hands may result in injury for which the owner could be held to blame. It is obviously difficult to prescribe a suitable magazine which must be portable, weather-proof and yet not easily broken open or removed bodily. One scheme used successfully in Western Australia is a locked metal-clad box bolted onto or beneath the floor of a truck or utility. Another employs a small drum on its side under a mound of earth, or perhaps kept in an excavation below surface. Always locate the explosives a reasonable distance - at least 50 feet for amounts up to 50 lb. - from men at work or rest. Detonators must also be treated with respect by storing similarly to, but never with, explosives, although the number required at first is usually too low to justify special arrangements other than providing a small box which could perhaps be kept in the vehicle, and supplies drawn as required.

PRECAUTIONS

Although explosives in good condition will not ignite of their own accord, fire is always regarded as a grave menace which may, however, be minimized by clearing scrub from the vicinity, and avoiding accumulations of wrapping paper or other burnable matter. Don't smoke near the explosives, when charging holes, or making up rods and primers, and avoid using open-flame kerosene and acetone lights.

DEFECTS

Modern explosives are manufactured to a high standard of safety and reliability, and by rigid inspection every effort is made to ensure continued perfection. Once in the consumer's possession, however, the explosive lies less within official control, and from this point onward its performance is largely dependent on the manner of storage and use. Even under ideal conditions, certain changes tend to make most explosives progressively less serviceable. It is, therefore, well to avoid over-ordering, and to use present supplies before opening a new lot. Of the several types of spoilage commonly experienced, ahsorption of moisture is the most likely. Loose plugs from an open carton or case should be kept in a lever-lidded can such as a gallon paint tin, but notwithstanding this precaution and the protective waxed wrapper, damage may occur. It can be very troublesome in a humid tropical atmosphere and where storage is in a damp mine or unventilated dead-end. Plugs in good condition are uni- formly firm to the touch, but if they show a marked contrasting softness for more than about an inch at one or both ends, or if droplets appear on pressing, their use is inadvisable. In such state they will not do the work expected of fresh explosive and; what is worse, sometimes become insufficiently sensitive to fire others in the same hole, leaving unexploded butts. On the other hand, the prospector may come across sticks of explosives which are too hard for proper tamping or insertion of the detonator. Here again bad storage is usually to blame. If once-wet explosive is baked out during summer in an unshaded iron magazine it may finish up about as hard as the rock it is intended to break. Another fault, happily rare nowadays, is exudation which, simply described, is a running-out or migration of nitroglycerin. It may result from a defect in composition and is always intensified by undue heat. The first sign is an oily film, spreading in bad instances to the paper lining and even onto the box. This is a dangerous state because the separated nitroglycerin is so "touchy" that even pushing a plug down a shothole could cause premature explosion. Finally, sticks of explosive are occasionally distorted or out-of-round, making charging difficult. They should not be forcibly pressed home hut gently rolled to restore their original cylindrical form. With a few plugs the position in storage does not matter, hut case lots should be kept so that the sticks stand up and are therefore not subjected to pressure from above layers. This applies particularly in hot climates. As for detonators and fuse, there is little that can go wrong provided the basic principle of cool dry storage is practised. Detonators should be clean and bright on the metal shell and show a well-defined indentation inside due to the die used in filling. If, through rough handling, the composition appears loose or powdery an accident could occur. Fuse should be prevented from kinking or bruising and must not be allowed to contact water, oil or petrol. Even if afterwards dried, its stand- ard burning rate of 80 to 100 seconds per yard may alter, become erratic or actually stop, causing a misfire. Pro- longed exposure to the sun or other high temperature source has much the same effect by liquefying the water-proofing compound which then penetrates the gunpowder train. Fuse thus mistreated cracks readily and may become useless for damp or wet work.

DISPOSAL OF EXPLOSIVES

"Dangerous or unserviceable explosives should not be left in the hush, buried or thrown into water. They are best got rid of by burning under supervision of an inspector of mines or explosives, or a member of the manufacturer's technical staff. All such officers are pleased to assist and advise, but should none be in the district, it is better for the prospector to take action himself rather than to put the defective explosive aside and perhaps forget it. The usual method of destruction is first to choose an open remote spot where the sticks of explosive are laid out in criss-cross fashion two or three deep in a line or train on newspaper, sprinkled with kerosene (not petrol) and lit at one end against the direction of the wind. By using a roll of burning paper, the operator can get well away before the fire takes hold. Generally, the whole lot burns to a harmless ash, hut as explosion may occur, everyone must stand well clear behind cover. For obvious reasons, detonators should be kept apart from fracture under destruction; any believed defective are best destroyed by tying to a sound one fired as usual, taking care to shelter from flying metal fragments. No special precautions are necessary in disposing of fuse which, together with trimmings or odd ends too short for use, may simply be tossed into a camp fire."

PREPARING EXPLOSIVES FOR USE

Assuming now that the prospector's explosives and accessories are in good order, the next step in preparation for blasting is to make up a primer, or that plug which when detonated will communicate explosion to the whole charge. From the outer end of the fuse coil, cut and discard an inch before measuring the length required, remembering that the burning rate is 80 to 100 seconds per yard, or about half a minute per foot. Make quite sure of ample time to reach a safe place after lighting, particularly when working underground, where never less than three feet of fuse is considered necessary. The cut should be made straight across and not on the slant, using either a sharp knife or special crimper-cutter tool obtainable for a few shillings. Next, a single detonator is removed by the fingers from the tin and inspected for sawdust inside. Any found usually falls out on gently shaking the open end ; its removal with a pin, match, wire or similar object may be highly dangerous. Then, avoiding twisting or forcing, slip the freshly-cut fuse into the detonator until it just touches the composition, after which the metal shell is crimped or closed onto the fuse with pliers or the tool just mentioned applied about an eighth-inch from the mouth or open end. Do not exert pressure anywhere other than this point. Now open the wrapper at one end of the explosive by a wooden skewer or pointed stick, which is then used to pierce the explosive itself. Pass the detonator into the hole thus made so that only the fuse is uncovered, turn back the paper and tie with string, taking a couple of loops around the plug. The result is a satisfactory primer from which the detonator cannot readily be pulled to cause a misfire.

CHARGING THE SHOTHOLE

Before charging, the hole should first be scraped clean of borings and dirt. Without slitting or breaking the wrapper, place a plug at the bottom and press home with a wooden rod. Introduce the next one, press it also firmly but gently into position and continue in this manner until the charge considered necessary has been added. Now lower the prepared primer, cover with about three inches of sand and tamp lightly, adding more and well ramming with the rod until the hole is completely filled.

This final tamping and the avoidance of air spaces in the explosives column are important because a loosely-placed poorly confined charge will not do its proper work. A good tamping or stemming mixture consists of sand and moist clay, but sand alone, earth, rockdust or whatever similar material is on hand will generally answer. Burnable stuff like paper, shavings, cotton waste, etc., should not be used, especially underground.

PLACING THE PRIMER

Some experienced miners put the primer at the bottom of the hole upside down, so to speak, with the detonator lowest of all and the fuse curved round to lie parallel with the length of the plug. While this practice has certain advantages, it is of course not workable unless the hole is wide enough to take the fuse alongside the explosive. Whatever position is adopted, the closed end of the detonator should always point into the column of explosive to be fired. The reason is that as most of the "kick" in a detonator fans out from the end, the effect in the opposite direction may not be sufficient for a satisfactory result. Therefore, place the primer with its detonator at the top or bottom of the shothole, and do not put detonators into plugs on the skew.

FIRING

This takes us to the final stage or actual firing of the charge. A couple of minutes before attempting to blast, the operator must not only give warning by calling "Fire" in a loud voice, but should personally see that everyone is at a safe distance and that all explosives surplus to the job are well clear. The surest way to light fuse is by the lighters sold for the purpose. A match flame is uncertain unless the fuse end is slit to expose the powder. A method which seldom fails, even in a strong wind, is to hold the match head firmly against the end and stroke the side of the box smartly across.

DANGER AFTER FIRING

All explosives on firing produce varying amounts of poisonous fumes of which the gas carbon monoxide is particularly treacherous because it has no smell, colour or taste. Being much the same density as air, it tends to "hang" rather than rise or fall. The fume danger is considerahly lessened in surface or open cut blasting, hut after using explosives in mines or other confined spaces no one should attempt an immediate return. A strong jet of compressed air is a satisfactory means of getting rid of the foul dusty atmosphere and for maintaining fresh conditions around the operator. For small mines without compressor or blower, natural ventilation assisted hy a windsail fitted to deliver fresh air onto the face where explosion has occurred will have to be relied upon, hut even so about eight hours should elapse before work is resumed. To play safe and yet avoid wasting time, the obvious way of going about blasting is to fire last thing before knocking off in the late afternoon.

FAILURE TO EXPLODE

If a charge fails to explode, keep clear of it for several hours, for apart from the fume danger there is sometimes a delayed action due perhaps to fuse accidently pulled from the detonator causing the wrapping paper to smoulder. The writer recalls an instance where one missed hole from a round fired about 5 p.m. went off in the early hours of the following morning. It is unwise to draw or interfere with a charge which has exploded incompletely or not at all. The recommended plan is to bore another hole parallel to and about a foot away, charge, fire, and in due course thoroughly search the broken stone for the detonator and pieces of explosives. Any such remnants should be destroyed in the manner already outlined.

NORTH BY THE WATCH

In Australia and in the rest of the Southern Hemisphere, when finding North by the watch, the figure XII is pointed at the sun. Use a watch showing approximately the right time. Place it in full sunlight so that a line through VI and XII will point to the sun. Note the direction of the small hand, Halfway between XII and the position of the small hand is North - that is a pencil lying along the centre, and the halfway will point to North. This method is not to be used within an hour of noon. The watch when used to give direction should be placed on a flat place.

HEALTH HINTS

The prospector or the man whose work carries him far afield away from civilisation has to face certain dangers to his health, for which he should be prepared.

He must find water where he can.

He must exist upon food easy of transport and mostly canned, and go without many fresh articles of food so necessary to health, and in many areas of this State cope with myriads of flies and other insects which are so apt to contaminate and spoil his food.

Finally he is responsible for his own sanitation, and if careless or callous, risks the dangers associated with the improper disposal of the wastes from his own body and the refuse from his camp.

A few hints in regard to these matters, therefore, may be of value to him :-

Water.-Man can live for many days without food, but for very few without water. Water, however, especially if he must take what he can get, is very subject to pollution. It may be contaminated by the discharges from the human body and so carry the germs of typhoid fever, dysentery, and diarrhoea. It may be contaminated by the dead bodies of birds and animals and contain poison from their putrefying bodies, and so be the cause of severe sickness. Even good water carried in tanks and water bags, if not kept covered, may be similarly contaminated by dust or by careless handling. The water supply, therefore, should be protected from such pollution by every means possible, and especially should the discharges from the human body be buried far from it and immediately covered with at least eighteen inches of soil and so located that the ground does not slope or drain towards the source of water. Where there is any suspicion that water may be polluted, it should be boiled before it is consumed.

Food. For perfect health a mixed diet is necessary, and when possible it should include starch contained in bread, potatoes, and the cereal grains; *Fats* contained in meats (especially bacon), butter, eggs, chocolate, nuts, and milk ; *Proteins* contained mainly in bread, meat, fish, cheese, eggs, milk, beans, and peas; *Mineral salts* in meat, grains, green vegetables, and fruits; the health-giving substances known as *Vitamins* mainly in milk, butter, grains, fruits, and fresh vegetables.

The starches and fats mainly produce heat and energy; the proteins are the building materials of the body for growth and repair; the mineral salts are necessary for blood and bone and the various secretions and juices of the body, and the vitamins prevent diseases such as scurvy, beriberi, rickets, and keep up the resistance of the body against septic infections and infectious disease.

It will be seen, therefore, how necessary is a mixed diet containing all of these. Porridge, canned orange or lemon juice, butter, cheese and marmite are particularly valuable foods.

When food becomes contaminated by dirt and flies, it may putrefy, ferment, or produce infectious diseases or ptomaine poisoning. It should, therefore, be kept covered at all times, and so far as possible be kept cool. If canned foods are "blown" that is, if the ends of the can bulge outwards and gas under pressure rushes out when they are punctured, the contained food is either fermenting or putrefying, and should not be eaten.

Sanitation.- A proportion of people carry in their bowel the germs of typhoid fever, dysentery, and diarrhoea, so that the bowel discharges are a source of danger to others, as these germs may be carried from their discharges to water or food by flies and dust.

It is, therefore, essential that in establishing a camp the first care should be to set aside, remote (i.e., not nearer than 50 yards) from the camp and the water supply, an area where the bowel discharges and the urine should be buried, and there should be no delay in covering this offensive matter, as flies may in a few minutes carry it to food or water, and so infect it with the diseases mentioned above.

The same careful removal or burning of refuse and food scraps from the camp should he carried out, as these not only attract flies, hut, if left lying about, act as breeding grounds for them.

Of some of our men out in the Mulga it is stated that they are lined with boiler plate - they drink such strange water without apparent ill-effect. We others should not expect a miracle every time we slake a thirst. If we must swallow fever germs, let us boil them first. Boil every drop of drinking water. Camps are kept cleaner than they used to be, on the average. But do not let us trust to averages, hut to boiled water and clean camps.

FIRST AID HINTS FOR PROSPECTORS

It is always advisable that prospectors should have a knowledge of First Aid, particularly if they are engaged in inspecting old workings, where there may be a danger from accumulations of poisonous gases or from loose ground or broken timbers. Every possible precaution should be taken to guard against accident, but should one occur, attention by a First Aid man may be themeans of saving life or limb, and of preventing perhaps a minor injury from developing into something serious. Haemorrhage should always receive first attention, as an injured person may die from loss of blood, whilst a fractured hone is not usually dangerous to life.

In the case of an artery being cut, pressure should be applied between the heart and the wound at a point where the artery crosses a hone. Points at which pressure may he applied to arrest bleeding may be felt by the heat at several parts of the body.

1. The Temporal Artery is directly in front of the opening of the ear.

2. The Facial Artery on the lower jaw hone about one inch from the angle of the jaw.

3. The Occipital Artery about three fingers breadth from the centre of the hack of the ear.

4. The Subclavian Artery behind the middle of the collar bone, pressure being applied downward and backwards against the first rib.

5. The Brachial Artery passes along the inner border of the biceps muscle ·and may be compressed by passing the fingers over the inner part of the muscle and pressing the artery close to· the bone.

6. The Radial and Ulnar Arteries pass along the inner and outer borders of the wrist and can best be compressed about one inch above the wrist, using the thumb after first elevating the injured arm.

7. The Femoral Artery passes along a line from the centre of the groin to the back of the inner side of the knee. Its beat may be plainly felt in the centre of the groin, and it should be compressed by the ball of the thumb at right angles to the surface against the bone of the pelvis.

If bleeding is severe a tourniquet should be applied by placing a hard substance, such as a stone, cork or a block of wood in a bandage around the limb. Take a tie in the bandage and, placing a short stick over the tie, tie again; the stick should then be twisted until bleeding ceases. The wound should be cleaned and dressed with antiseptic dressings and a thick pad placed over the wound and secured with a bandage tied tightly. The tourniquet may then be loosened but should not be removed. Should bleeding recommence the tourniquet should be tightened again but relieved slightly about every half-hour until a doctor's services have been procured.

To guard against contamination by germs from flies, dust, etc., all cuts and wounds, no matter how small, should be painted with tincture of iodine.

FRACTURES

A simple fracture is one in which the bone is broken but the skin remains intact.

A compound fracture is one in which the skin is broken allowing germs to enter the seat of fracture.

A complicated fracture is one in which other organs such as an artery or an internal organ (the liver, lungs, spleen, etc.) have been ruptured by the broken hone or hones.

In case of fracture the patient should be treated on the spot. Extreme care should be taken in handling the fractured part, as careless handling may result in converting a simple fracture into something more serious.

General treatment for fractures is by splints and bandages. Improvised splints may be made out of any rigid article, such are the bark of a tree, a sapling, tin, or cardboard.

Do not remremove the clothing unless the fracture is compound or complicated. In the latter cases the wound should be cleaned and dressed, after which the splints should be applied firmly to the limb by securing the splint above the fracture first and then below and adding several bandages consisting of whatever material may be at hand, to insure safety in transport. In case of a broken leg, tie it to its fellow (after securing with splints) if the patient has to be transported.

BURNS

Burns are usually associated with severe shock, and care and tact must be used in dealing with the patient. In case of burns remove the clothing with extreme care, to prevent breaking any blisters, and dress the burnt part with lint or clean linen which has been soaked in bicarbonate of soda (baking soda) solution; a teaspoonful of the soda to a pint of boiled water. If picric acid or acriflavine is available, it may be used as an alternative. Bicarbonate of soda solution is highly recommended for all burns and scalds, and should be applied by soaking lint in the solution, placing this on the affected part, covering with cotton wool and securing with bandage.

FUMES AND POISONOUS GASES

In these cases the patient generally becomes unconscious and the pulse is very weak. Artificial respiration should be resorted to at once, and when consciousness is restored an emetic should be given in the form of one table-spoonful of mustard in a large tumbler of water slightly warm, or two tablespoonfuls of salt in warm water. Stimulants such as hot strong tea or coffee should be given and the patient kept warm.

GENERAL

In all cases of accident the patient should be treated for shock by applying warmth and stimulants until the services of a doctor have been obtained.

Stimulants should on no account be given, however where bleeding cannot be controlled, or in the case of severe injury to the head, or where a patient is found unconscious.

ARTIFICIAL RESPIRATION

The victim of fumes and poisonous gases should be brought into the air at once. Anything in his mouth likely to become an obstruction such as false teeth, tobacco, food, etc., should he removed at once. Begin artificial respiration at once. Do not wait to loosen the patient's clothing. In Artificial Respiration proceed as follows:-

(a) Lay the patient on his stomach, with arms extended forward, and with face to one side. Let an assistant draw forward the patient's tongue. See that the nose and mouth are free for breathing.

(b) Kneel straddling the patient's thighs, and facing his head; rest the palms of your hands on the loins (on the muscles of the small of the back), with fingers spread over the lower ribs.

(c) With arms held straight, swing forward slowly so that the weight of your body is gradually, not violently, brought to hear. This act should take from two to three seconds.

(d) Then immediately swing backward so as to remove the pressure, thus returning to the former position. See (b) above.

(e) Repeat deliberately twelve or fifteen times a minute the swinging forward and back - a complete respiration in four or five seconds.

(f) As soon as this artificial respiration has been started and while it is being continued, an assistant should loosen the patient's clothing about his neck, chest and waist.

Continue the artificial respiration if necessary two hours or longer, without interruption, until natural breathing is restored or until the doctor arrives.

If natural breathing stops after being restored, use artificial respiration again.

Do not give any liquid by the mouth until the patient is fully conscious. Give him fresh air but keep him warm.

Where anyone is overcome underground by poisonous fumes, would-be rescuers are warned that if they enter the danger zone immediately, they will become victims and so increase the difficulties of the position. If compressed air is available a ready and safe course is to take an air hose to the scene of the mishap. In the absence of compressed air probably it will be desirable to tie a rope to any rescuer so that if need be he may be hauled back. In any case ropes should be carried so that the man overcome may be drawn to the surface.

Prospectors and miners are advised to realise and study the problems of rescue from zones of poisonous gas.

WARNING

It may be, necessary to warn some readers that the fumes of mercury, or of roasting ore, or of acid treatments are highly dangerous, and should not be breathed, Most dangerous of all are the aromatic fumes from solid cyanide or cyanide solutions or precipitates and the fumes of "white arsenic" that are given off by arsenical gold ores when they are roasted. When work involving fumes has to be carried out, it is better to operate in the open air, or in a forced draft, so that the wind will carry away fumes as they form.

The breaking down of sulphuric acid with water is a possible source of danger. Great heat is engendered, and splashes of the hot mixture can cause very painful wounds.

Great care should be taken in handling Nitric Acid. It should not be poured into an iron vessel. Beware of splashes, as nitric is severe on clothing and on the hands and face.

Certain Minerals are occasionally mistaken for gold:

(1) pyrite, iron pyrites; (2) copper pyrites; (3) bismutite, carbonate of bismuth and bismite, oxide of bismuth; (4) limonite or iron hydroxide in a form exhibiting yellow irridescence; (5) mica in some forms; (6) lead chromate. Gold is to he distinguished from all these minerals by its weight and malleability. Gold is so dense that it hangs behind in the dish when samples are panned off. Small specks of gold in auriferous ore can be distinguished from other yellow metallic minerals, as named above, because gold yields, without crumbling, to the touch of a needle or the point of a knife. All of the minerals named crumble fairly easily and most of them change colour on heating to redness or the application of acid.

CHROMATE OF LEAD

If the prospector places some of the tail formed in the panning dish on a suitable hard surface, say a penny or a knife, and rubs it with a knife blade, gold will polish and chromate will powder.

DECEIVING THE PROSPECTOR

Lead chromate deceives so many prospectors, that one of our State Battery managers suggests a routine to be adopted in certain districts when panning off a sample. Let the sample be taken rather larger than usual. Dolly and divide it into two parts. Roast one part on a sheet of iron over a fire. Now pan off each part separately.

If the "tail" of gold seems the larger in the unroasted part, suspect lead chromate. Lead chromate often offers an appearance of gold likely to mislead experienced men. Another aid to this deception is that lead chromate is heavy and " hangs " in the dish. Roasting changes its colour and greatly reduces its power to deceive. Sometimes one is deceived by the brass from cartridge cases, melted in old camp fires, and found after the ashes have disappeared, or by the scratch of a brass boot nail on an exposed rock.

THE OLD PROSPECTOR

The revival of interest in gold mining is marked by the rediscovery of old prospects and workings rather than by the establishing of new fields. Surface indications were energetically taken advantage of by the old prospector, and in spite of improved transport and facilities, it is seldom that we hear of likely country that has not been examined by him. What a wonderful man he was! Assailed by thirst, hunger, weariness, he never admitted defeat. Something of a hermit, he shunned his fellow men-something of an ascetic, he despised the shelter of towns-something of a mystic he walked beneath a rainbow nobody else could see, secure in the faith that he would presently find the crock of gold!

SCIENTIFIC PROSPECTING

Exploration by the latest scientific methods is now practised. Photographs of vast stretches of country are made by aeroplanes fitted with the latest photographic and wireless apparatus. Ground staffs of geologists and draftsmen co-operate in the production of geological maps. In chosen spots there will be geo-physical examinations followed by diamond drilling. The operations are assisted by a hopeful combination of large capital, business management, and science. Prospecting expeditions have never before commanded such technical equipment, or worked to such a plan of campaign. Every unusually heavy mineral found by a prospector should be submitted to the School of Mines or the Government Chemical Laboratory. Heavy minerals are often valuable.

GOLD PLUS SILVER

Gold is seldom or never found without an admixture of silver. In a few extreme cases the proportion of silver in the bullion has been large enough to be a handicap to the mine.

STRAKING

Straking is a process of catching the gold on cloth or fabric, corduroy being the most used at present. The cloth is laid on a plane surface which can be tilted to the required slope. The cloth is removed at intervals and washed in a tub to remove the adhering gold. Actually a little of the gold will not be removed by washing and ultimately the cloth has to be burned and the ash treated.

Strake cloth is usually laid on thick sheets of fibrolite set at a slope of 1½ inches to the foot. The coarser the pulp the steeper the slope. The area of cloth varies from one to two square feet per ton of ore per 24 hours and the pulp should hold about ten times as much water as ore.

Corduroy strakes will catch gold that amalgamation would miss either because the gold has some covering to prevent amalgamation, or the ore fouls the plates.

On the other hand, the concentrate is bulky and requires further treatment. It is ground with water and lime in an amalgamating barrel or Berdan pan for several hours. Then mercury is added and the grinding continued for an hour or more. The pulp is thinned, run over riffles to catch the amalgam, and the tailings reserved for cyaniding.

SULPHIDE TREATMENT PLANTS

There are two types at present operating in Westem Australia.

1. Fine grinding and straight cyanidation. If coarse gold is present it is usually recovered by strakes in the grinding circuit.

2. Fine grinding and flotation followed by roasting and cyaniding of the flotation concentrates. If the flotation tailings contain sufficient gold they are also cyanided. Coarse free gold may be recovered by strakes.

The type of plant most suitable for a particular ore has to be ascertained by experiment.

SULPHIDE ORE

Sometimes a small mine unexpectedly runs into sulphide ore and the owner is at a loss what to do next. It is usually out of the question to establish a special plant, and even then it would be necessary to learn which of several systems it would be best to adopt. Expert advice must be sought. For instance, a sample of the sulphide ore could be sent to the School of Mines,

Kalgoorlie, to ascertain whether ordinary State Battery treatment would give satisfactory extraction. If State Battery treatment is not suitable, it may be possible to make arrangements for one of the larger mining companies to take the ore.

BANKING

Some prospectors and leaseholders who strike gold commence to have financial worries almost immediately. Where a prospector sells direct to a Bank, and has a surplus over his immediate needs, he should open an account. A current account, with one's own cheque book, is very useful as long as there is a credit balance. The Bank may be at Perth or Kalgoorlie or the home town, or where the stores are purchased - distance does not matter very much. The proceeds of gold can be sent anywhere, and easily (perhaps too easily) drawn out by cheque. The prospector may deal with a Savings Bank Agency. These agencies are numerous and have been a boon to many a man outback. For the man who is shy about opening an account in a Bank or a Savings Bank - let him remember that there is always difficulty and anxiety about money stored in a camp.

FOR THE TRADE

For the convenience of the Trade, the Mint keeps on hand a small supply of gold and silver strip.

SLAGS, ETC., FROM BULLION

Slags from gold melting are liable to contain shots of gold, possibly very minute. The slags may be finely ground and then panned off. Panning should be "not too close," i.e., the pan should be used to make a concentration of the heavier portions of the slag. The concentrates can be put in the crucible and run down with a little added borax. If this is poured into a mould placed on an iron plate, the mould will catch most of the gold, and the slag will overflow on to the plate.

SIZE OF FIRST CRUSHING

Prospectors opening up a lease are sometimes dis- appointed with the results of the first crushing. It is possible to send in 100 tons and find the values eaten up by the cost of cartage. In many cases prospectors would be well advised to make their first crushing not larger than fifteen or twenty tons.

PUBLIC CRUSHING FACILITIES

Although there are still a few privately owned small treatment plants for gold ores in working condition, the cost of crushing is so high that few would be interested in crushing for the public. Public crushing facilities for small producers of gold ores are therefore almost entirely confined to the State Batteries.

State Batteries for treating gold ores at at:

Bamboo Creek	Coolgardie
Marble Bar	Kalgoorlie
Nullagine (Sandy Creek)	Norseman
Peak Hill	Yarri
Meekatharra	Ora Banda
Cue	Menzies
Mt. Magnet (Boogardie)	Leonora
Sandstone	Laverton
Payne's Find	Lake Darlot
Marvel Loch	

PROSPECTING SUCCESSES 1958

"Golden Key" in the Boulder centre during 1956-58, crushed 499 tons for 529 fine ozs. gold, including 47 ozs. dollied.

"Leslie " at Wombola, 1958, from 118 tons produced 110 fine ozs.

"Rosemary " also at Wombola, 1958, crushed 286 tons for 648 fine ozs.

"Rayjax " at Bonnievale in the Coolgardie Goldfield, for 1958 crushed 70 tons for 135 fine ozs.

P.A. 7101 at Eundynie has produced 200 fine ounces from 4 tons of ore and dollied gold.

"Sons of Erin" at Higginsville has crushed 57 tons ore and recovered 170 fine ozs., including 75 ozs. dollied.

P.A. 7107 at Red Hill, in September, 1958, crushed 8 toris of ore for 31 fine ozs.

At Coolgardie itself, the Camel Paddock (or Camp) still produces thrills in the way of rich dabs.

At Kunanalling the " Resolute" goldmine in June, 1958, crushed 4.50 tons for 9.71 fine ozs.

In the Lawlers goldfield, the " Goanna " Find on Wildara Station has so far produced 104 fine ozs. of alluvial gold.

From the Black Range Goldfield, the "Dingo" gold mine in February, 1958, crushed 1 ton of ore and recovered 202 fine ozs. gold.

"Leslie" at Wombola	118 tons	110 fine ozs.
"Bluebird" at Yaloginda, Meekatharra	60 tons	83 fine ozs.
"Wheel of Fortune South," Lennonville, Mt. Magnet	18 tons	51 ozs.
"Eclipse Mine", Mt. Magnet	2,840 tons	2,942 ozs.
P.A. 2614Z, at Mt.Ida, Menzies	12 tons	22 fine ozs.
"Hazel Dawn" at Ullaring	8 tons	11 ozs.
"Golden Wonder" at Ullaring ..	90 tons	462 ozs.
"Fourmile" Gold Mine at Mulwarrie	8 tons	34 ozs.
"Oakley" Gold Mine at Mulwarrie	300 tons	283 ozs.
P.A. 1692R at Yerilla	14 tons	21 ozs.
"S.H.E." Gold Mine at Gindalbie	116 tons	101 ozs.
P.A. 2597T at Duketon, Mt. Margaret	19 ozs. of Alluvial.	
P.A. 2416, The New Find at Beete, Dundas	9 tons	16 ozs.
P.A. 2417, The New Find at Beete, Dundas	10 tons	19 ozs.
P.A. 2372 in the Norseman District	70 tons	84 ozs

TIN ORE

Tin ore; cassiterite, may be recognised among the heavy black minerals by the following test: The only materials required are some commercial hydrochloric acid, which is mixed with an equal amount of water before use, and a zinc dish or hollowed zinc block. The test should he done in the open to avoid breathing the acid fumes given off. Place the pieces of mineral in the dish or the hollowed portion of the block and pour diluted acid into the dish or block to a depth of about one quarter of an inch. A vigorous evolution of gas should commence immediately. Wait until all the action appears to have ceased. Rinse several times with water to remove the acid and then examine the pieces of mineral. Any pieces of cassiterite present will he found to have been coated with a surface layer of metallic tin.

USE OF CORDUROY

In Western Australia the collection of free gold on corduroy tables is only practised where amalgamation is not undertaken, that is, hy the mines which crush in cyanide solution and the treatment consists of fine grinding and cyaniding, or fine grinding, concentration by flotation and cyaniding. In the treatment of ordinary free-milling ores, there is no evidence to suggest that the use of corduroy is preferable to amalgamation either in percentage recovery or convenience in collecting the gold. i.e., the clean-up. In the treatment of sulphide ore, especially that containing sulphides which may sicken the mercury, the corduroy table may be superior to amalgamation. Practice at Kalgoorlie suggests that a table 28 inches wide by 10 feet long should he ample on taking the pulp from a five-head mill. The table could be made twice this width and divided in the centre, so that the pulp can he directed to one side while the corduroy blankets on the other are being washed. For ordinary output, the fall in the table could he 1¼ inches to the foot, or sufficient to prevent the sand from accumulating on the corduroy. As with the ordinary battery practice, about a ten per cent. pulp should be suitable.

DENSITY OF METALS

A cubic foot of pure platinum weighs 1,330 lb., pure gold 1,205 lb., pure silver 655 lb., lead 710 lb., copper 550 lb., cast-iron 450 lb., tin 455 lb., aluminium 165 lb. These weights are in avoirdupois, and are approximate.

The ounce avoirdupois is smaller than the ounce troy. Thus, 100 ounces troy equal 109.71 ounces avoirdupois. "From ounces avoirdupois take ten per cent. to get ounces troy," is a rough and ready rule for small quantities. In Mint returns weights are expressed in troy ounces and hundredths of an ounce-pennyweights and grains are not used.

PROSPECTING FOR ECONOMIC MINERALS

Apart from its evasiveness in payable quantities gold is probably the most satisfactory metal from the Prospector's point of view. It is easily recognised, treatment facilities are usually available and there is an immediate market at a fixed price - at the nearest Bank for all that can be produced, whether the quantity be great or small.

Most other minerals do not come into this category and as a general rule a market has to be sought for them. The price is often a matter of arrangement between producer and consumer and in many cases a regular output must be guaranteed before any contract to supply consumers can be finalised.

The size of this publication does not permit a description of the many minerals of potential importance which may be met by the prospector in his search for gold. It is well for him to bear in mind, however, the possibility of discovering a mineral deposit, which, if properly handled, may be of more value to him than a gold prospect.

Unfortunately, few economic minerals are as easily recogisable as gold, while others, of which mica and quartz crystals might be quoted as examples, are quite easy to recognise as such, but may be of little value owing to their small size or certain physical defects and flaws.

Beryl is a mineral, a constituent of many pegmatites which is easily enough recognised when found in the usual flat-topped hexagonal crystals, or in some of its characteristic blue and green colours. When broken, however, and bleached or milky, or of a whitish, pinkish, or other non-characteristic colour, it is often difficult to distinguish from quartz or felspar.

Any mineral which is unusually heavy is generally of interest; Black minerals of this type such as tantalite, wolfram or possibly cassiterite (tin ore), might be casually picked up and discarded as "ironstone pebbles." The prospector is advised should he find a mineral which is strange to him, or ore which he believes to contain any metal in economic amounts, he should submit it to the Government Chemical Laboratories, Adelaide Terrace, Perth.

These Laboratories will identify such specimens and, if justified, will analyse them to determine their quality or grade. These identifications and assays are free under the same conditions as gold on page 46. A covering letter should be forwarded with the specimens and any Inspector of Mines or Mining Registrar will be glad to assist the prospector avail himself of this service.

It might be thought that a list of minerals with market prices against them should be published here, but, owing to the fact that the prices vary considerably from time to time, such a list could be very misleading.

In addition, a number of minerals are penalised for certain impurities, thus causing further variation in price, while some are not accepted if their assay is below a certain minimum standard.

It will be seen that, even when a certain mineral has been determined as such, careful sampling and assaying are necessary to determine its value.

Prospectors are again urged to submit any unusual minerals for determination and in so doing they may not only enrich themselves, but may possibly sow the seeds of a new industry in the State.

Men holding Golden Eagle nugget, Kalgoorlie, Western Australia, Jan 1931
(Museums Victoria)

MINES DEPARTMENT OF WESTERN AUSTRALIA

The Mines Department establishment at Treasury Buildings, cnr. St. George's Tee., and Barrack Street, Perth, is as follows :---

Hon. Minister for Mines Under Secretary for Mines

Asst. Under Secretary for Mines

State Mining Engineer

Chief Coal Mining Engineer

Superintendent of State Batteries

Inspector of Explosives

Chief Draftsman

Principal Registrar

Government Geologist, Geological Survey of Western Australia, cnr. Beaufort and Francis Streets, Perth.

Director, Government Chemical Laboratories, cnr. Adelaide Terrace and Plain Street, Perth.

Deputy Chief Inspector of Machinery, Inspection of Machinery Branch, 108 Adelaide Terrace, Perth.

Inspector of Machinery, Burt Street, Boulder.

Director, School of Mines, Kalgoorlie.

Officer-in-Charge, School of Mines, Norseman.

Officer-in-Charge, School of Mines, Bullfinch.

Inspectors of Mines - Kalgoorlie, Cue, Collie.

Workmen's Inspectors of Mines - Kalgoorlie.
    Leonora.
    Cue.
    Port Hedland.
    Collie.

Mining Registrars - Bridgetown. Meekatharra.
Broome. Mount Magnet
Carnarvon. Norseman.
Collie. Northampton
Coolgardie. Onslow.
Cue. Ravensthorpe.
Hall's Creek. Southern Cross
Kalgoorlie. Marble Bar
Leonora.

Officers of the Department are always pleased to help prospectors, especially new men and men in strange Fields.

Inspectors of Mines and Departmental Geologists are constantly in the field and will readily assist prospectors on the spot whenever possible.

WEIGHTS AND MEASURES

The abbreviation for cubic centimetres is "c.c,"

1 gallon water	= 277.274 cubic inches
8 pints = 1 gallon	= 10 lb. avoirdupois
1 ton water	= 224 gallons
1 cubic foot water	= 62½ pounds
1 cubic foot quartz	= 164 pounds
1 cubic foot lode-stuff	= 170 to 200 pounds
1 pint	= .568 litres
480 grains = 20 dwts.	= 1 ounce troy
7,000 grains = 16 ounces	= 1 pound avoirdupois
39.370 inches	= 1 metre
.039 inch	=1 millimetre
315 inches	= 8 metres
1 inch	= 25.399 millimetres
1 mile	= 1.6093 kilometres
1 cubic inch	= 16.387 cubic centimetres
1 grain	= .0648 grammes
8 grains	= .5184 grammes
1 pound avoirdupois	= .4536 kilogrammes
7.92 inches	= 1 link
100 links	= 1 chain = 22 yards
10 square chains	= 1 acre = 4,840 sq. yds.
22 yards x 220 yards	= 1 acre
44 yards X 110 yards	= 1 acre
12 chains X 20 chains	= 24 acres

GLOSSARY

ACID ROCKS.- Igneous rocks containing a high percentage of silica.

AMPHIBOLITE.- A metamorphic, in places schistose, rock, with hornblende as the chief constituent and with subordinate felspar.

ANTICLINE.- An arch-like fold of strata having a long axis so as to form a ridge instead of a dome.

ASBESTOS.- A general name given to a number of fibrous non-combustible silicate minerals, usually white, grey or greenish grey in colour. The chief varieties are chrysotile, crocidolite (blue asbestos) and anthophyllite. The fibres should be easily separable, strong, fine and silky.

BASALT.- Usually a fine-grained basic igneous rock which has been cooled on the surface of the earth as a lava flow. A basalt, however, may never reach the surface before cooling.

BASIC ROCKS.- Igneous rocks containing a comparatively low percentage of silica.

BAUXITE.- Aluminous laterite. Ferric oxide, silica and titanium oxide are present in varying amounts. Used in the production of aluminium.

BERYL.- Silicate of beryllium and aluminium. Colour various, may be green, blue, yellow, grey or white. Often found as well crystallised hexagonal prisms. Sometimes shows striations due to parallel growth. When showing no signs of crystallisation, it is difficult to distinguish from quartz. Flawless transparent crystals are valued as gem stones. Chief ore of beryllium.

BISMUTITE.- A basic carbonate of bismuth of variable composition. Cream colour; earthy. Ore of bismuth.

BLOCK FAULTING.- The breaking and moving of large portions of the earth's crust, by which distinct blocks of varying height are formed.

"BLOWS."- A local term applied to prominent hills of quartz and ironston.

BREAKAWAYS.- A local term applied to the steep cliffs connecting old and new plateaux. The top of the cliff is usually capped by laterite, below which the rocks are decomposed.

BRECCIA.- A rock composed of angular fragments of pre-existing rocks, consolidated by some cementing material, such as silica, carbonate of lime, etc. The constituent rock fragments may be formed by the ordinary agents of weathering or by the crushing force exerted by great earth movements.

CASSITERITE (Tinstone).- Oxide of tin. Heavy (specific gravity, 6.9). Commonly found in river gravels as black pebbles.

CEMENT.- A local term indicating a tough rock which in some places is "wash" cemented together by silica or other material, and in other places is decomposed bedrock hardened by the same material.

CHALCOPYRITE (Copper Pyrites).- Sulphide of copper and iron. Colour, brass yellow. Surface tarnishes readily, sometimes becoming irridescent, when it is known as peacock ore.

CHERT.- A common typo of chalcedony, which is a form of oxide of silicon.

CLAY.- A general name for the fine aluminous sediments that are plastic.

CONGLOMERATE.- A rock composed of pebbles rounded by water action or by earth movements, nod cemented by ferruginous, calcareous silicious or other material.

COSTEANING.- Says the Century Dictionary: "The general direction of the lode having been, us supposed, approximately ascertained by means of work already done, the object of the costeaning is to trace the lode still further through ground where its outcrop is not visible on the surface." This is not the Australian interpretation. If the lode is believed to run North and South the costean usually takes the form of a trench running East and West. It is an exploratory trench whose width and length are determined by the circumstances.

CROCOITE.- Chromate of lead. Colour, various shades of red. Soft. A minor constituent of some ores. Being heavy and bright, has been mistaken for gold by prospectors when panning.

DEEP LEADS.- As used in Western Australia, this term means old stream channels, which have become so buried beneath the waste of the land that the channels no longer act as drainage lines.

DEFORMATION.- The folding, fracturing, faulting and warping of the earth's crust by earth movement.

DIABASE.- A basic igneous rock frequently occurring in sheets or dykes. Broadly speaking, it may be called an altered dolerite. One of the "greenstones."

DOLERITE.- A dark coloured basic igneous rock consisting largely of augite and felspar. One of the "greenstones."

DOLOMITE.- A rock of mineral consisting of carbonate of lime and magnesia.

DYKES.- Bands of generally vertical or nearly vertical igneous rocks, which traverse other rocks and which are thin in proportion to their length and depth.

EPIDIORITE.- An altered "greenstone" rock now consisting of hornblende and felspar.

FAULT.- A fracture in the earth's crust, along which one or both of the adjacent rock masses has or have moved.

FAULT PLANE.- The surface along which the rock masses have moved during the formation of a fault.

FELDSPAR- Group name. Silicates of aluminium with varying amounts of lime, potash and soda. The chief varieties are microcline (potash feldspar), plagioclase (soda-lime feldspar) and albite (soda feldspar). All feldspars cleave easily in two directions nearly at right angles, splitting with even, smooth and shiny surfaces. Used in ceramic industry.

FLUORITE (Fluorspar).- Fluoride of calcium. A glassy mineral of many different colours. Usually well crystallised in the cubic system. Sometimes massive. Easily scratched. Used as a flux.

FOLDED ROCKS.- Rocks which, by movements within the earth's crust, have been thrown into a series of arches and troughs of a widely varying character.

FOLIATIONS PLANES.- A series of approximately parallel close-set planes in a rock mass, by which minerals are arranged in distinct lines, and the rock acquires an appearance somewhat like the edges of a book.

GABBRO.- A basic igneous rock generally of deep-seated origin and composed of augite and felspar.

GALENA.- Sulphide of lead. Generally in blue-grey masses or cubic crystals. Soft, metallic lustre, and a perfect cubic cleavage. May carry rich silver values. The principal ore of lead.

GNEISS.- A rock generally similar in composition to a granite but having its component minerals arranged in definite layers or " folia." A gneiss is a metamorphic rock and may result from either a sedimentary or an igneous rock.

GRANITE.- A crystalline rock consisting essentially of quartz and felspar grains with any of the following minerals present in minor proportions : Biotite mica, muscovite mica, or hornblende. The Western Australian goldfields granites usually consist of quartz and felspar with some biotite mica,.

GREENSTONE.- A field term applied to more or less altered rocks which have a characteristic dark green colour due to the presence of the minerals chlorite, hornblende, epidote, etc. It may be either schistose or massive.

HAEMATITE.- Any anhydrous oxide of iron.

HAEMATITE-QUARTZITE.- A metamorphic rock commonly occurring on the goldfields of Western Australia composed chiefly of haematite and quartz. Frequently referred to as "Jaspar Bar " or "Banded Iron Formation."

HORNBLENDITE.- A rock consisting almost wholly of hornblende plates or prisms and containing no felspar.

IGNEOUS ROCKS. - Rocks which have originally been in a molten condition and have cooled either on or within the earth's crust.

JASPER.- Opaque chalcedony of red, brown, yellow or green colour. frequently applied to the Banded Iron Formations.

JOINTS.- Cracks or partings in a rock distinct from bedding or cleavage planes.

LATERITE.- A term used in Western Australia to indicate the hard cap on granite and other rocks, such cap having resulted from the decomposition of those rocks. Laterite may be predominantly ferruginous, aluminous or silicious.

LAVA.- A rock which in a molten state has issued from vents or fissures and which solidifies on· or close to the surface of the earth.

LIMESTONE.- A rock composed mainly of carbonate of lime. Most limestones have been formed in the sea by the accumulation of the hard parts of marine animals and plants.

LIMONITE.- Hydrous oxide of iron. Of widespread occurrence. Commonly brown ; massive. Colour ranges from yellow to nearly black. Ore of iron and constituent of most soils and as a brown staining en many minerals.

MANGANESE.- Manganese minerals seldom occur· singly, but usually as mixtures in association with limonite. Manganite, polianite, psilomelane and pyrolusite are all oxides of manganese; black in colour. They vary from soft and earthy to hard and massive.

Manganese oxide forms as a black stain on many minerals.

MARL.- An earthy and usually soft form of limestone.

MICA.- Group name for various silicate minerals characterised by a perfect basal cleavage whereby they readily split into thin elastic sheets. Muscovite (potash mica) and phlogopite (magnesian mica) occur in large transparent or slightly stained sheets highly valued for their electrical insulation and heat resistance properties. Lepidolite (lithia mica) is ore. of lithium. Biotite (black mica) has no commercial value.

MOLYBDENITE.- Sulphide of molybdenum. Usually as small soft bluish-black scales with a bright metallic lustre. Strong resemblance to graphite. Leaves a bluish-grey trace on paper. Ore of molybdenum.

PYRITE (Iron pyrites).- Sulphide of iron. Pale, brassy to golden yellow in colour. Usually in granular masses or grains; sometimes as well crystallised cubes. Sometimes called "new chum gold." May occasionally carry gold values. Commercial source of sulphur in the manufacture of sulphuric acid.

PYROXENITE.- A granitoid, non-felspathic rock, the chief mineral of which is pyroxene. It contains no olivine.

QUARTZ.- A common form of oxide of silicon. There are many varieties. Rock crystal is the purest form.

QUARTZ PORPHYRY.- An acid igneous rock closely related to granite, but generally found in dykes and small masses; contains round or nearly round quartz crystals up to half inch diameter.

QUARTZITES.- Metamorphic rocks formed almost wholly of silica grains. They are of various origin.

ROCK HOLLOW.- A hollow or cave cut more or less horizontally beneath a hard rock cap or at the foot of a lake cliff of hard rocks.

ROCK WEATHERING.- The general term applied to all natural methods by which a rock is broken up and decays.

SANDSTONES.- Rocks composed essentially of compacted, usually quartz, sand. The character of the rock may vary according to the cementing material, such as iron, lime, etc.

SCARP.- The face forming a sharp transition from a higher to a lower belt of country. It may be due either to erosion or faulting.

SCHEELITE.- Calcium tungstate. Colour variable, commonly white to greenish-yellow. Usually as granular masses of scattered grains. Fairly heavy (specific gravity, 6.1). Ore of tungsten.

SCHISTS.- Metamorphic rocks (with a predominant mineral such as mica, hornblende, etc.) which split along approximately parallel lines.

SEDIMENTARY ROCKS.- Rocks which have been formed as sediments or deposits under water. Wind-blown deposits (aeolian rocks). are generally included in this series, notwithstanding their inability to fit the definition. .   .

SHALE.- A sedimentary clayey rock, which splits along the original planes of deposition.

SHOAD.- The word "shoad," sometimes spelt "shode," means "floaters," or loose fragments of ore mixed with earth, lying on or near the surface and indicating the proximity of a lode. "Shoading" is a word in use in some mining districts and is the process of searching for valuable ore by collecting and examining loose stones on the surface or slightly buried in the soil. The expression "shed-ore" is more often heard than "shoad-ore," and more likely to be understood by the prospector.

SILL.- A sheet of volcanic rock injected between layers of other rocks.

SLATE.- A clayey rock which splits into thin plates at various angles to the bedding.

SPHALERITE (Zinc blende).- Sulphide of zinc. Colour varies, commonly brown. Generally in cleavable, fine to coarse granular or compact masses. Brittle; resinous to adamantine lustre. Chief ore of zinc.

STRATA.- The series of successive deposits one above the other which compose a sedimentary rock.

STRIKE.- The general trend or direction in a horizontal line of a lode, stratum or fault.

SYNCLINE.- A trough-shaped curve of strata, having one long axis, which distinguishes it from a basin.

TANTALITE-COLUMBITE.- The minerals of this group are tantalates and niobates of iron and manganese. They form a continuous series grading from tantalite (the iron tantalite) through mangano-tantalite (the manganese tantalite) and columbite (the iron niobate) to mangano-columbite (the manganese niobate). They are heavy black minerals, somewhat resembling cassiterite. Specific gravity varies from 7.9 tantalite to 5.2 columbite. Tantalite is the chief ore in the production of tantalum.

URANINITE (Pitchblende).- Mainly oxide of uranium. Source of uranium and other radioactive elements. The pitchblende variety is usually black and pitch-like in appearance.

WEATHERING.- The decomposition, disintegration and breaking up of the earth's crust by the action of changes of temperature and of rain, wind and frost.

WOLFRAMITE (Wolfram).- Tungstate of iron, and manganese. Generally as thick tabular or bladed crystals. Colour usually black with, a brilliant metallic lustre. Heavy (specific gravity, 7.4). Ore of tungsten.

ABOUT THE AUTHOR

Hugh Annan Corbet was born in East Ballarat, Victoria in 1870. He started out as a junior clerk in the Melbourne branch of the Mint and was first employed at Perth Mint in 1898.

He was the first Chairman of the Melville Road Board, appointed in 1901. He was among the first residents of Duncraig Road, in Melville Water Park Estate and was Chairman on that board 1908-12.

During WW1, Major Corbet (88 Perth Infantry) worked with the Intelligence Section of the General Staff in Perth.

He moved into the residence attached to the Perth Mint in 1926 and held the position of Deputy Master of the Mint from August 1928 until 31 December 1934.

Major Corbet wrote a popular booklet *Hints to Prospectors and Owners of Treatment Plants* in 1932, at a time when the price of gold had risen and many were seeking it.

Major Hugh Corbet stands here,
Who can tell you why sovereigns
     are dear,
  For, down at the Mint,
  Where the bullion bars glint,
  He is able to tell by a squeeze
     and a squint
Why alloy puts the gauge out of
     gear.

From Ballarat came he to Perth
When an ounce was but 80 bob
     worth,
  But since those far days
  They have managed to raise
  The price of the quids which
     auriferous blaze

The price of the quids which
     auriferous blaze
That rules in most parts of the
     earth.

A book on prospecting is his,
Which no one can question or
     quiz,
  And if many young chaps
  Would pack up their traps,
  And roll the old bluey inside
     of their straps,
For the Mint there'd be plenty
     more biz.

ETT IMPRINT has the following ION IDRIESS books in print in 2024:

Prospecting for Gold (1931)
Lasseter's Last Ride (1931)
Flynn of the Inland (1932)
The Desert Column (1932)
Men of the Jungle (1932)
Drums of Mer (1933)
Gold-Dust and Ashes (1933)
The Yellow Joss (1934)
Man Tracks (1935)
Over the Range (1937)
Forty Fathoms Deep (1937)
Madman's Island (1938)
Headhunters of the Coral Sea (1940)
Lightning Ridge (1940)
Nemarluk (1941)
Shoot to Kill (1942)
Sniping (1942)
Guerrilla Tactics (1942)
Trapping the Jap (1942)
Lurking Death (1942)
The Scout (1943)
Horrie the Wog Dog (1945)
In Crocodile Land (1946)
The Opium Smugglers (1948)
The Wild White Man of Badu (1950)
Outlaws of the Leopolds (1952)
The Red Chief (1953)
The Silver City (1956)
Coral Sea Calling (1957)
Back O' Cairns (1958)
The Wild North (1960)
Tracks of Destiny (1961)
Gouger of the Bulletin (2013)
Ion Idriess: The Last Interview (2020)
Ion Idriess Letters (2023)
Walkabout (2024)

www.ingramcontent.com/pod-product-compliance
Lightning Source LLC
Chambersburg PA
CBHW041110110426
42740CB00054B/3444